IN THE EAGLE'S EYE
YELLOWSTONE

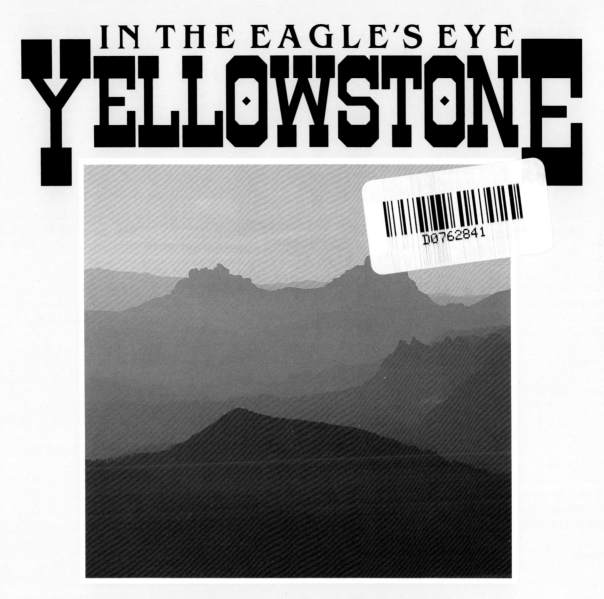

A Collection of Aerial Photography
by Larry Mayer of the Billings Gazette
Introduction by Robert Barbee
Foreword by Wyoming Gov. Mike Sullivan

Published by The Billings Gazette
Wayne Schile, Publisher
Richard Wesnick, Editor
Photos by Larry Mayer, Chief Photographer

©1991, *The Billings Gazette*, A Division of Lee Enterprises

Library of Congress Catalog Card Number 91-071321.
ISBN 0-9627618-2-6.

For extra copies of this book contact:
The Billings Gazette, P.O. Box 36300, Billings, Montana 59107-6300.
In Billings, call 657-1200. Or call toll free from outside Billings 1-800-927-2345.

Book Design by Tom Waterman.
Cover Design by Ben D. Leonard.
Printed by Fenske Printing Inc., Billings, Montana.

Photo Captions by Robert Ekey.
French Translations by Daniele Nisewanger.
German Translations by Michael Clow.
Japanese Translations by Kazuyo Hayashi Erickson.

Printed in the U.S.A.

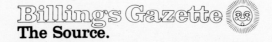
Billings Gazette
The Source.

INTRODUCTION

ROBERT D. BARBEE

In America's continuing quest to care for its natural heritage, Yellowstone Park has been one of our greatest teachers. The park, with its complicated ecological personality and its many geological wonders, has compelled us to think, sometimes harder than we might have liked to, about nature and our place in it. The spectacular aerial images of Yellowstone in this book reveal yet another way, one of many, in which we can learn from this wild country.

The traditional way to appreciate a national park, and the most highly recommended for Yellowstone, is from the ground: hiking, driving, camping, fishing and doing all the other things the park offers us. But even from high above, Yellowstone can be enjoyed and can offer fresh lessons about its character and its beauty. Once you've gotten used to the bright colors and striking patterns of these pictures, look for the stories the pictures tell.

The stories are all about change. The complex and remarkably variable processes that have given us today's Yellowstone still are hard at work, and their effects are often very easy to see.

The easiest changes to see are those involving the park's life forms. About one third of the park's vegetation was affected in one way or another by fires in 1988; the evidence of those burns will be a major feature of the Yellowstone landscape for decades, until the new generation of forest, born in the ashes, replaces the snags and fallen trees with a new blanket of green. That process already has completed itself in the meadows, and a walk through the woods reveals that it is well under way there, too. From the air, the jigsaw patterns of burn and non-burn show the subtle ways in which fire creates and maintains a variety of habitats across such a giant landscape.

But change operates on many timetables here, and most of them are longer than the life of a tree. For example, the sweeping curves of shoreline along the islands in Yellowstone Lake reveal much about the prevailing wind patterns and wave actions that shape those islands. The shallow, braided delta waterways of that same lake tell us how the steep slopes of surrounding mountains are very gradually being relocated in the shifting wetlands of the lake shore. Wind and water continue to sculpt Yellowstone as they have for millions of years.

There are much greater changes in evidence, though. Yellowstone's turbulent geological history is evident in many places. Again, look at Yellowstone Lake. The immense circular bay we call West Thumb, and the smaller Mary Bay are both the result of gigantic geothermal explosions long ago. Hayden Valley, a grand meadowland northwest of the lake, is the former bed of another lake that left its richer sediments there and allowed the valley to become a productive grassland surrounded by less-fertile forests. To the west, the series of irregular white stone patches is the site of the world's foremost collection of geysers, where hot water, emerging mineral-laden from far below, is creating new rocks and new landscapes every day. Yellowstone has been a restless landscape for a very long time.

These long-range perspectives may make today's visitors seem insignifcant by comparison, but even humans, who have occupied the Yellowstone region for 10,000 years at most, have had their effects. Park developments and roads are visible in many pictures. Though extensive alterations of the natural setting are restricted to lands near a few major attractions, these alterations must always be watched carefully to make sure they don't unduly affect the ecological process that people come to see. A campground or other development may seem relatively small when driven through, yet look startlingly large when seen all at once, with all of its carefully designed little byways visible. Accommodating the needs of park visitors and managers without letting those needs diminish the wonders that the visitors come to see always has been the foremost challenge facing the National Park Service. Seeing Yellowstone's human developments from the air makes it clear how serious a challenge that is.

There are many ways to enjoy these pictures. They are nature's answer to abstract art, vast flowing patterns of light and dark, height and depth, darkest shade and most brilliant reflection. They are portraits of pristine forests, subalpine lakes and steep canyons. They are chapters from the land's geological and ecological biographies, with new chapters being written even as the airplane circles overhead.

If they are also, as I believe, a test of our care in using the land, then they are a revealing testament to how much we have loved it; for most of it looks much as it would have if someone had flown over it with a camera 200 years ago.

Robert D. Barbee
Superintendent
Yellowstone National Park

FOREWORD

GOV. MIKE SULLIVAN

Most of us who have been fortunate enough to spend much time in Yellowstone National Park continue to search for ways to see more of this magnificent natural resource, and from different perspectives.

Perhaps that is why we climb the park's mountains, hike or ski its backcountry trails, canoe its waterways or return to marvel at Old Faithful in different seasons or times of day.

We seek to experience each unique feature of this national treasure from every conceivable angle. And we dream. When we can't reach those inaccessible vantage points, we let our thoughts wander to the wonders spread before us.

We imagine ourselves as the first humans to encounter this strange, steaming land of geysers and hot pools that to the untrained eye has changed little in centuries, yet is undergoing constant change.

The Grand Canyon of the Yellowstone, for example, today looks very similar to its now historic portrayal by early Western artist Thomas Moran more than a century ago. Yet change in the geothermal areas has been striking, with new geysers being discovered each year while others go dormant.

One of my dreams has always been to be an eagle, soaring above Yellowstone, seeing it from that perspective.

A few summers ago, I was waist deep in the Yellowstone River, practicing the relaxing ritual of fly-casting, when I gazed up and saw a bald eagle soaring quietly in the warm afternoon thermals, gliding effortlessly about me and the river. I began wondering what that eagle was seeing from its lofty perspective.

What would it be like, I wondered, to cruise the air currents far above the park, seeing the endless blue ridges of mountains and silvery, serpentine streams meandering through sun-splashed green meadows?

What would the elk, bison and bears look like from the air? Could I spot a grizzly sow teaching her cubs to fish? Could Morning Glory Pool be any bluer from the sky or the canyon any more golden?

Did that eagle realize it was looking down at Yellowstone National Park, the world's first national park and the crown jewel of our national park system? An important symbol of our nation's commitment to preserve and protect our environment? A world-class attraction for visitors and a source of enormous pride for those of us who reside in the three states that border the park?

It was another very special Yellowstone experience for me. A common experience for the eagle, probably, but certainly unique to a Wyoming lawyer spending a restful summer afternoon pursuing dreams and fish.

We residents of Wyoming, Montana and Idaho are particularly blessed because Yellowstone encompasses parts of our states. We think of it as our park—not in terms of ownership, for we know this park belongs to all people and to the ages, but in terms of our stewardship of the park.

It was this special relationship with Yellowstone that caused us to personally grieve as we witnessed the forest fires of the summer of 1988. It once again impressed upon us the intimacy of our relationships with this treasure and, as well, the awesome raw power of nature.

Wyomingites, Montanans and Idahoans are fortunate because our proximity to Yellowstone affords us easier opportunity to see it from different perspectives and vantages, to know its different moods and characters, to understand and cherish its living things and their importance to the natural order.

We can—and do—return to Yellowstone again and again to explore it in different ways and to see different parks. Just as the neighboring Tetons take on different character in each change of time, light, shadow and season, so too does Yellowstone.

Nothing is as stimulating as witnessing the quiet majesty of Yellowstone in winter, unless it is seeing its rebirth each spring or hearing the calls of bugling elk in the fall.

We are a friendly lot here in the West, with a camaraderie born of the pioneer spirit and the cowboy humorist. We are proud of Yellowstone and its surrounding areas, and we love to share our perspectives of the park with visitors.

Whatever your interest, we stand ready to direct you to a new vantage point, a new way of seeing Yellowstone.

Perhaps your interest is in the geological oddities, the world's most concentrated collection of geysers, hot springs,

Photo by Fred Yates

3

and mud volcanoes. Perhaps it is the diverse wildlife, the magnificent, free-roaming big-game animals found throughout the park or, like my wife Jane's special interest, Yellowstone's prolific and colorful native plants and wildflowers. Perhaps it is the outdoor experience—the fishing, hiking, camping, skiing or snowmobiling.

Perhaps your interest is historical, envisioning the shock of nomadic Indian tribes or first white trappers who visited the park and couldn't quite believe their eyes. John Colter was one of those. When he returned to "civilization" in St. Louis, people didn't believe his tales of what they called "Colter's Hell."

To me, it is the spectacular beauty, the clean air and water and the natural inhabitants. But most of all, it is the inspirational power of this incredible place.

I recall another special Yellowstone experience a few winters ago, when a group of us stood huddled together on a cold, crisp moonlit night waiting and watching Old Faithful. Just before midnight, Old Faithful erupted, sending its steaming water into the starry nighttime sky, and another wondrous performance began. A few minutes later, as Old Faithful's timeless magic ended and the last of its receding waters flowed across the cone, the sky behind the geyser erupted with nature's fireworks—the Northern Lights.

When I returned to "civilization" a few days later, like John Colter, nobody believed me, either. But I know. I was there, and from that perspective, I saw something in combination that very few people have seen.

I am equally fortunate to have this opportunity to be a part of "Yellowstone in the Eagle's Eye" and to join you in seeing the park through the unique perspective of Larry Mayer's art. It may be the closest we will come to being eagles.

Whatever our perspective, Yellowstone offers a unique adventure, and those of us who consider ourselves Yellowstone's stewards are delighted to share its mysteries and beauties with you. We invite you and, indeed, urge you to visit Yellowstone and witness its grandeur from your own perspective.

Wyoming Gov. Mike Sullivan

ABOUT THE PHOTOGRAPHER

LARRY MAYER

"Yellowstone In The Eagle's Eye" is the second book of aerial photography created by Larry Mayer, award-winning chief photographer of The Billings Gazette.

The first, "Montana From The Big Sky," captured the stunning beauty and vastness of the state known as the Big Sky Country. "Yellowstone In The Eagle's Eye" sweeps across the breathtaking panorama of Yellowstone National Park, the "crown jewel" of all national parks.

"Montana From The Big Sky" and "Yellowstone In The Eagle's Eye" are the outgrowth of Larry Mayer's love of photography and his love of flying. The photographs in these books were taken from the cockpits of his two planes, a Cessna 180 and a Cessna 172.

Mayer joined The Billings Gazette in 1977. His work has appeared in The New York Times, Geo, Time, Newsweek, U.S. News and World Report, American West, Associated Press, United Press International, National Wildlife, National Geographic World and National Geographic's book on Yellowstone National Park.

Additionally, he contributed to other recent books, including "Montana On My Mind," which was published by The Billings Gazette and Falcon Press, and to "Yellowstone On Fire!," "The Big Drive," and "Wagons Across Wyoming" which were published by The Billings Gazette.

The captions for this book were written by Robert Ekey, a Bozeman-based writer who is intimately familiar with and who has written extensively about Yellowstone National Park.

The publisher would like to express his appreciation for the assistance and cooperation extended by the National Park Service which graciously granted permission for Larry Mayer to shoot aerial photographs of Yellowstone.

Yellowstone National Park

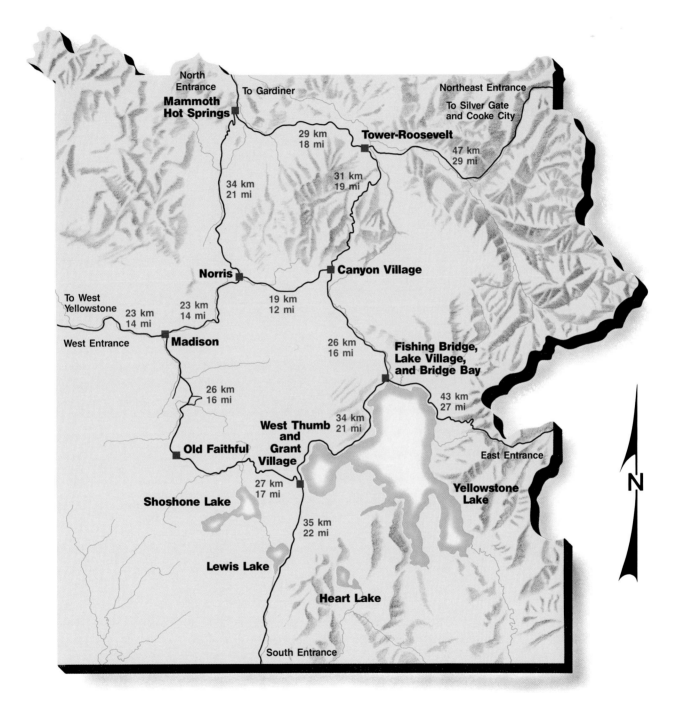

The shadows from lodgepole pines on Stevenson Island streak across a shimmering Yellowstone Lake at sunset.

Les ombres des pins à l'Ile Stevenson dessinent des traces ondoyantes sur le Lac Yellowstone qui scintille sous le soleil couchant.

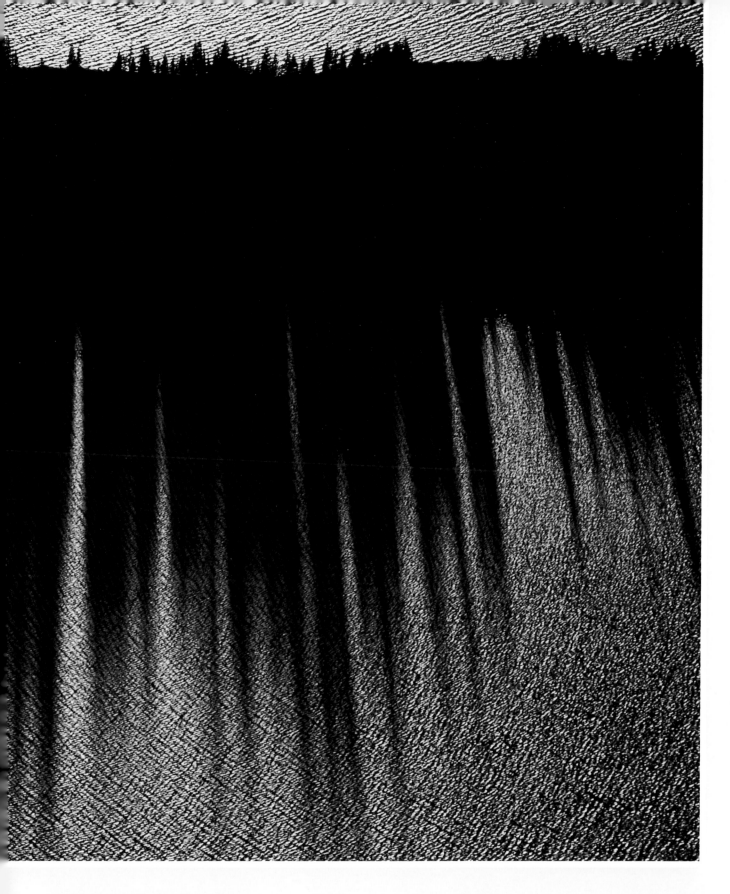

Die Schatten von Drehkiefern auf der
Stevenson Insel streifen bei Sonnenuntergang
den schimmernden Yellowstone See.

日没時、スティーブンソン島に茂
るロッジポール松の影がイエロー
ストーン湖にながくなげかかる。

Tower Falls est une chute de 40 mètres de haut près de la Rivière Yellowstone. Un rocher de la taille d'une voiture, perché précairement en haut de la cascade, a poussé bien des gens à prédire sa chute. Il est tombé en juin 1986.

Bei *Tower Falls* in der Nähe des Yellowstoneflusses fällt Wasser 40 Meter in die Tiefe. Ein wagengroßer Felsblock befand sich einmal am Rande der Fälle und verursachte dabei Mutmaßungen über sein Hinabfallen. Das Felsbrockenwahrzeichen fiel endlich im Juni 1986 hinunter.

イエローストーン川近くにあるタワー滝が40メートルの高さから落下する。かって滝の崖淵に車大の玉石がすわっており、いつそれが落ちるかといろいろ言われてきたが、このランドマークも1986年の六月ついに滝へ落下した。

Tower Falls plunges 132 feet near the Yellowstone River. A car-sized boulder once perched at the brink of the falls, prompting various predictions on when it would fall. The landmark boulder toppled off the falls in June 1986.

La neige recouvre le sommet imposant de *Turret Mountain* (la Montagne à Tourelle) dans le sud-est de Yellowstone. La roche volcanique de la chaîne des Absaroka contraste vivement avec la neige fraîche.

Schnee bedeckt den beeindruckenden Gipfel des *Turret Mountain* (Turmberg) in der südöstlichen Ecke des Yellowstoneparks. Der vulkanische Fels des Absarokagebirges steht in starkem Kontrast zum neuen Schnee.

イエローストーンの南東隅にある人目を引くタレットマウンテェン（小塔山）の山頂に雪がかかる。アブサロカ山脈の火山岩が新雪と非常に対照的である。

Snow drapes off the imposing peak of Turret Mountain in the southeastern corner of Yellowstone. The volcanic rock of the Absaroka Range contrasts sharply with the new snow.

Ci et là, les couleurs d'automne décorent le bord du Lac Shoshone. On peut souvent voir des élans et des wapitis près du lac, qui est aussi un refuge pour les oiseaux aquatiques.

Herbstfarben kolorieren das südwestliche Ufer des Shoshonesees. Elche und Wapiti werden oft in der Nähe des Sees gesehen, der auch ein Zuhause für Wasservögel ist.

ショション湖西湖畔に秋の美景がみなぎる。この近くではムース（大鹿）やエルク（大鹿）がよく見られるし、水鳥の生育地でもある。

Autumn colors splash along the southwestern shore of Shoshone Lake. Moose and elk can often be seen near the lake, which also serves as home for waterfowl.

Des randonneurs traversent dangereusement près d'une source chaude à côté de *Queen's Laundry* (Lessive de la Reine) dans le *Sentinel Group* (Groupe Sentinelle) du *Lower Geyser Basin* (Bassin de Geysers du Bas). Il y a plus de cent ans, on y nageait et on y faisait sa lessive; ce n'est plus le cas aujourd'hui, il a été nécessaire de les fermer pour les protéger.

Wanderer nähern sich illegal einer heißen Quelle in der Nähe von *Queen's Laundry* (Wäscherei der Königin) in der *Sentinel Group* (Wachegruppe) des *Lower Geyser Basin* (Unteres Geiserbecken). Die Quellen dieses Gebietes wurden vor mehr als hundert Jahren zum Wäschewaschen und Schwimmen benutzt. Um sie zu schützen, sind diese Quellen heute nicht mehr zugänglich.

徒歩旅行者がローワー間欠泉域セ
ンチネルグループにあるクイーン
ズランドリー（女王の洗濯場）付
近の立入り禁止温泉地区に危険を
無視して入り込む。 この辺の温
泉は100年以上までには洗たくや
水泳に使用されたが今では閉鎖さ
れ保護されている。

Hikers illegally traverse dangerously close to a hot springs near Queen's Laundry in the Sentinel group of the Lower Geyser Basin. The springs in the area were used more than a century ago for laundry and swimming, but are now closed to protect them.

Chaque matin, l'Ile Stevenson semble s'étirer d'un bout à l'autre du Lac Yellowstone. Cette île, visible de *Lake Hotel* (l'Hôtel du Lac), est habitée par les aigles qui se nourrissent de truites, en abondance dans ce lac.

Die vom *Lake Hotel* (Seehotel) sichtbare Stevenson Insel scheint sich auf dem Yellowstonesee gemächlich auszustrecken. Auf der Insel lebende weißköpfige Seeadler fressen die zahlreichen einheimischen Forellen des Sees.

スティーブン島がイエローストーン湖に早朝の背伸びをしているかのように見える。レイクホテルから展望できるこの島には豊富にいるカットスロート鱒を餌にしている禿げ鷲が生育している。

Stevenson Island seems to take an early morning stretch across Yellowstone Lake. Visible from the Lake Hotel, the island is inhabited by bald eagles, which feed on the lake's abundant cutthroat trout population.

Le Parc de Yellowstone se ravive quand le soleil se montre sur les montagnes Absaroka et envoie ses rayons sur le Lac Yellowstone. On peut voir le Lac Stevenson en premier plan.

Yellowstone Park belebt sich, wenn die Sonne über dem Absarokagebirge aufgeht und ihre Strahlen auf den Yellowstonesee sendet. Stevenson Insel ist im Vordergrund.

太陽の光線がアブサロカ山脈の上に輝やき、イエローストーン湖にその光線を投げかけると、イエローストーン公園はまるで生き返ったかのように見える。前景に見えるのはスティーブン島である。

Yellowstone Park comes alive as the sun peaks over the Absaroka Mountains and showers its rays on Yellowstone Lake. Stevenson Island is in the foreground.

Le *Grand Canyon of the Yellowstone* (Grand Canyon de Roche Jaune) se situe en deuxième place comme attraction touristique du parc. Ici, la Rivière Yellowstone creuse son lit à travers la roche volcanique, créant un canyon de 1.200 mètres.

Eine 30 Kilometer lange 450 Meter tiefe Schlucht, der *Grand Canyon von Yellowstone*, , ist die zweitbeliebteste Sehenswürdigkeit des Parks. Hier hat sich der Fluß Yellowstone in vulkanisches Gestein eingeschnitten und einen 1 200 Meter breiten Riß verursacht.

亀裂の長さ30キロ、深さ450メートルに及ぶイエローストーンのグランドキャニヨンはイエローストーン公園で二番目に人気のある場所である。ここではイエローストーン川が火成岩を切開き幅1200メートルのキャニオンを創造している。

A fissure twenty miles long and 1,500 feet deep, the Grand Canyon of the Yellowstone is the park's second most popular tourist attraction. Here, the Yellowstone River carves its way through volcanic rock, creating a canyon 4,000 feet wide.

Les *Lower Falls* (Cascades du Bas) de la Rivière Yellowstone scintillent par des couches de nuages au lever du soleil. En hiver, l'eau plongeant en brume les 94 mètres vernit de glace les côtes du canyon.

Die *Lower Falls of the Yellowstone* (Untere Wasserfälle des Yellowstones) schillern bei Sonnenaufgang durch eine Wolkenschicht. Wasser, das 94 Meter in die Tiefe stürtz, verursacht einen Dunst, der im Winter zu Rauhreif wird und dann die Wände des Cañon bedeckt.

日の出には、イエローストーン川のローアーフォールズ滝（下の滝）が朝日を受けて雲間にきらきらと輝く。94メートルの高さから落下する滝は霧状の水しぶきを上げ、冬は谷の岩壁の表面に氷の結晶がでる。

The lower falls of the Yellowstone River sparkles through layers of clouds at sunrise. Water plunging the 308 feet over the falls sprays mist that, in the wintertime, covers the canyon walls with rime ice.

Le *Mud Volcano* (Volcan de Boue) et les *Dragon's Mouth Hot Springs* (Sources Chaudes de la Bouche du Dragon) sont des endroits qui attirent les visiteurs qui traversent la Vallée Hayden. Les trous de boue qui gargouillent contrastent avec l'ardeur des Sources Chaudes de la Bouche du Dragon.

Der *Mud Volcano* und die *Dragon's Mouth Hot Springs* (Schlammvulkan und Drachenmaul Heiße Quellen) sind beliebte Sehenswürdigkeiten für durch das Haydental fahrende Parkgäste. Die gluckernden Schlammsprudel stehen im Kontrast zu der wallenden Aktivität der *Dragon's Mouth Hot Springs*.

マッドボルケーノ（泥の火山）やドラゴンズマウス（竜の口）温泉池はヘイデンバレー（ヘイデン渓谷）を通って旅する公園の観光客に入気のある場所である。ぼこぼこと沸騰する泥沼池はドラゴンズマウス温泉の波立つ活動と対照的である。

The Mud Volcano and Dragon's Mouth Hot Springs are popular stops for park visitors traveling through Hayden Valley. The gurgling mud pots contrast with the surging activity of Dragon's Mouth Hot Springs.

Des voitures, des camions et des camionettes de camping font la queue à l'entrée ouest du parc de Yellowstone. Avec 40% des 2,5 millions de visiteurs qui entrent dans le parc par cette porte; c'est l'entrée la plus utilisée.

Fahrzeuge aller Art: Autos, Lastwagen und Wohnmobile, reihen sich in die Schlange am Westeingang des Yellowstoneparks ein. Als verkehrsreichster Eingang im ganzen Park, dient der Westeingang 40 Prozent der jährlich zweieinhalb Millionen Gäste.

自家用家、トラック、レクリエーション車がイエローストーン公園西入口に列をなしている。この入口は公園の中で最も賑わい 年間250万人もの観光客のうち40パーセントがここから入る。

Cars, trucks and recreational vehicles line up at Yellowstone's West Entrance. The busiest of all entrances, 40 percent of the park's 2.5 million visitors enter the park here.

Les motoneiges et les bisons ont l'air de connaître les régles de la route. Ici, les hommes et les bisons se partagent la route déblayée le long de la Rivière Madison. Les animaux sauvages profitent souvent des routes déblayées plutôt que de marcher dans la neige profonde.

Schneefahrzeugfahrer und Büffel scheinen die Verkehrsregeln zu kennen. Hier teilen Menschen und Büffel die gepflegte Fahrbahn entlang dem Fluß Madison. Wilde Tiere machen sich oft lieber die für Schneefahrzeuge gepflegten Straßen zunutze, als in tiefem Schnee zu gehen.

スノーモービルに乗る者とバイソン（バッファロー）の両方が道路の規則を知っているかのように見える。ここでは、マディソン川沿いの手入れされた道路を人間とバイソンとが共有している。野生動物も雪深いところをを歩くよりもスノーモービル（雪上車）の為に手入れされた道路をよく利用する。

Snowmobilers and bison both seem to know the rules of the road. Here, man and bison share the groomed road along the Madison River. Wildlife often take advantage of roads groomed for snowmobiles rather than walk in deep snow.

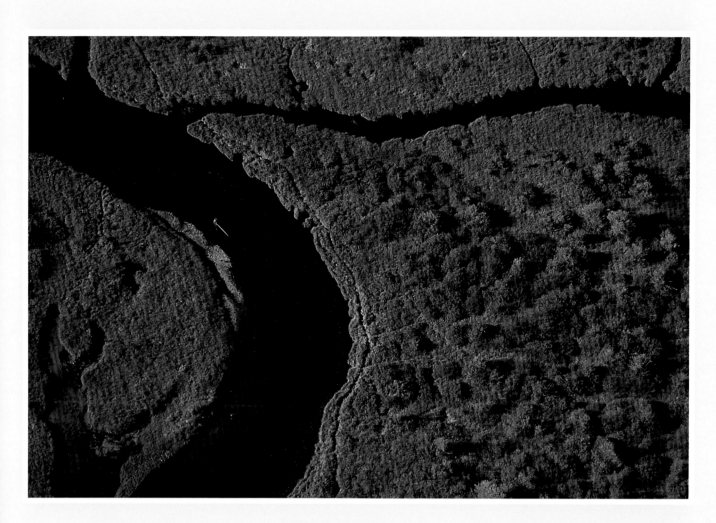

Un pêcheur à la mouche tente sa chance sur la Rivière Madison dans la section ouest du parc. Les rivières du Parc sont un paradis pour les pêcheurs à la mouche; ils y attrappent plusieurs types de truites.

Ein Fliegenangler im westlichen Teil des Parks wirft die Angel aus nach Forellen im Fluß Madison. Die Flüsse in Yellowstone sind ein Mekka für Angler, die Bach-, Regenbogen- und einheimische *Cutthroat* - Forellen fangen möchten.

フライフィシャーマンがイエローストーン公園の西方にあるマディソン川でますを釣っている。イエローストーンにある川はカットスロートます、ブラウンます、虹ますを釣るフライフィシャーマンにとって憧れの地である。

A fly fisherman casts for trout on the Madison River in the western portion of the park. Yellowstone's streams are a mecca for fly fishermen, who work the streams for cutthroat, brown and rainbow trout.

Les constructions adjacentes atténuent la grandiosité d'*Old Faithful* (le Vieux Fidèle), témoignant de sa popularité. *Old Faithful* fait éruption toutes les 50 à 100 minutes, son eau jaillissant jusqu'à 40 mètres.

Die Bebauung um den *Old Faithful* Geiser herum läßt ihn fast klein erscheinen. *Old Faithful* bricht in Abständen von 50 bis 100 Minuten aus und spritzt dampfendes Wasser durchschnittlich etwa 40 Meter in die Höhe.

観光客に人気のあるオールドフェイスフル間欠泉も回りにある建物の中では小さく見える。オールドフェイスフル間欠泉は50分ないし100分ごとに平均40メートルの高さに噴き上げる。

Development dwarfs Old Faithful, testimony to the geyser's popularity. Old Faithful erupts every 50 to 100 minutes, spraying water an average of 130 feet in the air.

L'eau, colorée par les bactéries, coule à partir du *Shoshone Geyser Basin* (Bassin des Geysers Shoshone) le long de la rive sud-ouest du Lac Shoshone. Dans ce bassin, seulement accessible par canoë ou à pied, on peut trouver des sources chaudes et beaucoup de geysers actifs.

Durch Bakterien gefärbtes Wasser strömt am südwestlichen Ufer des Shoshonesees aus dem *Shoshone Geyser Basin* (Shoshone Geiserbecken) heraus. Dieses schöne Gebiet kann nur zu Fuß oder mit einem Kanu erreicht werden und hat heiße Quellen und mehrere aktive Geiser.

バクテリアにより変色した水がショション湖南西岸沿いのショション間欠泉域から流れる。徒歩かカヌーでしか行けないこの域は温泉やいくつかの活間欠泉がある。

Bacteria-colored water flows off the Shoshone Geyser Basin along the southwestern shore of Shoshone Lake. Accessible only by hiking or canoe, there are hot springs and several active geysers in the basin.

Près de la bordure ouest du parc, la Rivière Madison se promène comme si elle ne savait quel chemin prendre. Cette rivière est renommée dans le monde entier pour la pêche à la truite et pour y voir des animaux sauvages.

In der Nähe der westlichen Grenze des Parks schlängelt sich der Fluß Madison entlang. Der Fluß ist wegen seiner Forellen weltberühmt und bietet eine ausgezeichnete Heimat für Tiere.

イエローストーン公園西境界近くのマディスン川がまるで迷い子になったかのように曲りくねって流れている。この川は野生動物の絶好な生育地であるし、また鱒は世界的に有名である。

Near the park's western boundary, the Madison River meanders as if unsure of what course to take. The watercourse offers excellent wildlife habitat, and is world-famous for its trout.

22

Des ruisseaux miroitent le long de *Firehole Lake Drive* dans le Bassin de Geysers du Bas. De la vapeur absorbée subitement bouillonne sous la surface de *Firehole Lake* et ressemble à des flammes d'où le lac a tiré son nom.

Im *Lower Geyser Basin* (Unteres Geiserbecken) entlang der *Firehole Lake Drive* (Feuerlochseezufahrt) schimmern Flüßchen. Der Feuerlochsee wurde nach dem zusammenbrechenden Dampf benannt, der unter seiner Oberfläche flammenartige Blasen bildet.

ローワーガイザーベイスン（下間欠泉盆地）にあるファイヤーホールレイクドライブ（火の穴湖車道）沿いに蒸気が光る。ファイヤーホール湖の水面下で落下する蒸気の泡立ちが炎に似ているところからこの湖にその名前がつけられた。

Streams shimmer along Firehole Lake Drive in the Lower Geyser Basin. Collapsing steam bubbling under the surface of Firehole Lake resembles flames and gave the lake its name.

Tongues of flame seem to dance around the 350-foot long Grand Prismatic Spring, Yellowstone's largest hot spring. The spectrum of brilliant colors is created by different types of photosynthetic bacteria, which vary according to water temperature.

Des langues de feu semblent danser autour de *Grand Prismatic Spring* (la Grande Source en Form de Prisme). Mesurant 100 mètres de longueur, cette source est la plus grande du parc de Yellowstone. La gamme de couleurs éclatantes est due à plusieurs types de bactéries photosynthétiques, qui changent selon la température de l'eau.

Flammen scheinen um die hundert Meter lange *Grand Prismatic Spring* (Große Prismatische Quelle) zu züngeln. Sie ist die größte heiße Quelle im Yellowstone Nationalpark. Die Palette von glänzenden Farben wird von mehreren Arten photosynthetischer Bakterien verursacht, die sich der Wassertemperatur nach unterscheiden.

小さな炎がその周囲を踊っているかのように見える長さ100メートルに及ぶグランドプリスマティクスプリングはイエローストーン最大の温泉である。色彩豊かに輝くスペクトルは温水の差による光合成細菌によってつくり出される。

Une crête très aiguisée mène au sommet d'*Amphitheater Mountain* (la Montagne en Forme d'Amphithéâtre) à une altitude de 3.297 mètres, il se trouve le long de la bordure nord-est du parc.

Ein schmaler Grat führt zur Spitze des *Amphitheater Mountain* (Amphitheaterberg), der 3 297 Meter hoch an der nordöstlichen Grenze von Yellowstone steht.

かみそりのように鋭く聳え立つ峰々がイエローストーン北東部境界線沿いにある標高3297メートルのアムフィシアターマウンテェン (円形山) の山頂へと連らなっている。

A razor-sharp ridgeline leads to the peak of Amphitheater Mountain, which stands at 10,847 feet along Yellowstone's northeastern boundary.

Des oxydes de minéraux variés donnent au Grand Canyon de Yellowstone ses couleurs jaune et orange vives. Le canyon lui-même est taillé dans la rhyolite et autres roches volcaniques atténuées par l'eau et les gaz chauds des régions thermales.

Verschiedene Mineralienoxyde rufen die glänzenden gelben und orangen Farben an den Wänden des *Grand Canyon* von Yellowstone hervor. Der Cañon selbst wurde in durch Wasser und heiße Gase weichgemachte Rhyolith und anderen vulkanischen Fels eingeschnitten.

各種の鉱石酸化物がイエローストーンのグランドキャニオンの岩壁を黄色やオレンジ色の極彩色にかえた。渓谷は熱水地帯からの水や高熱ガスによって柔かくなった火山岩が切り開かれたものである。

Oxides of various minerals create the brilliant yellows and oranges of the walls of the Grand Canyon of the Yellowstone. The canyon itself is carved in rhyolite and other volcanic rock softened by water and hot gases from thermal areas.

Mountain Creek (Ruisseau des Montagnes) se faufile à travers les montagnes boisées au sud-est du Parc de Yellowstone. C'est là que la Rivière Yellowstone prend sa source.

In der südwestlichen Ecke des Yellowstone Parks schlängelt sich *Mountain Creek* (Bergbach) durch die bewaldeten Berge, welche die Quelle des Flusses Yellowstone sind.

イエローストーン川の源水である山の小川がイエローストーン公園の樹木に覆われた山脈をぬうように流れている。

Mountain Creek threads its way through the forested mountains in the southeastern corner of Yellowstone Park, the headwaters for the Yellowstone River.

Une nappe de brouillard enveloppe le Grand Canyon de Yellowstone dès l'aube. Taillant son chemin à travers le plateau de Yellowstone, le canyon a souvent son propre micro-climat.

Eine Nebeldecke dunkelt den *Grand Canyon of the Yellowstone* (Großer Cañon von Yellowstone) gegen frühes Morgenlicht ab. Der in die Yellowstone Hochebene eingemeißelte Cañon bringt oft sein eigenes Klima hervor.

早朝のもやがイエローストーンのグランドキャニオンを一面に覆う。イエローストーン高原を連なる渓谷が時折その独特な微気象をうみだす。

A blanket of fog shrouds the Grand Canyon of the Yellowstone from early morning light. Carving through the Yellowstone plateau, the canyon often creates its own microclimate.

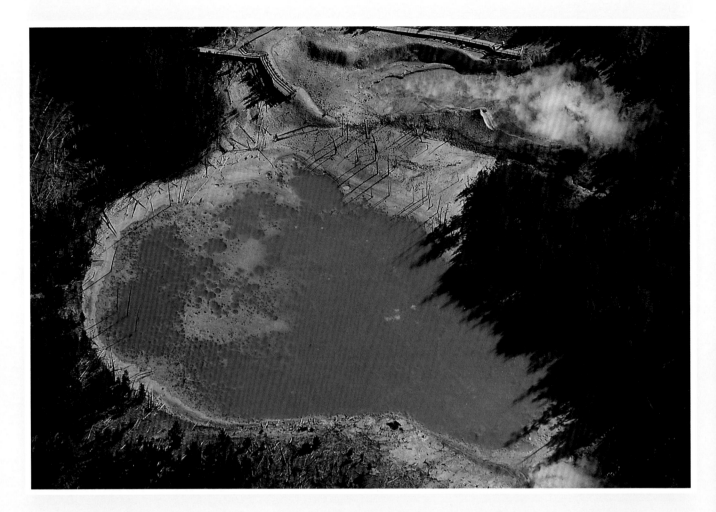

Sour Lake (le Lac Amer) couleur d'émeraude est adjacent au *Black Dragon's Caldron* (Chaudron du Dragon noir), un trou de vase bouillante qui a fait son apparition en 1948. Les spectateurs sont vraiment surpris par l'activité violente de cette vase noire à Black Dragon's Caldron situé dans la région du *Mud Volcano* (volcan de boue) près de Vallée Hayden.

Der smaragdgrüne *Sour Lake* (Saurer See) liegt neben dem *Black Dragon's Caldron* (Schwarzerdrachenkessel), einem Schlammsprudel, der 1948 plötzlich und explosiv ausbrach.

エメラルド色したサワー湖は1948年に爆発してできた泥地獄のブラックドラゴンスカルドロン地獄に隣接している。ヘイデンバレー（ヘイデン渓谷）近くのマッドボルケーノ（泥火山）地域にあるブラックドラゴンスカルドロン（黒竜大釜）地獄の強烈な音が観光客をぶきみがらせる。

Emerald-colored Sour Lake sits adjacent to Black Dragon's Caldron, a mudpot that exploded into existence in 1948. Visitors are awed by the violent agitation of the dark mud in Black Dragon's Caldron, located in the Mud Volcano area near Hayden Valley.

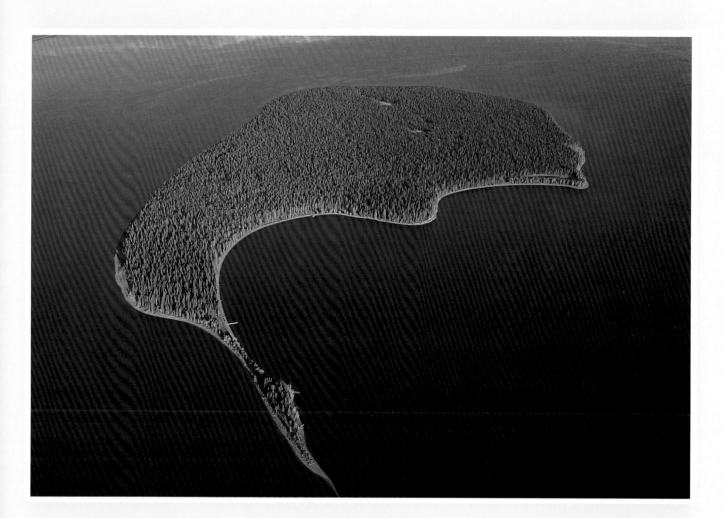

Frank Island (l'Ile Frank), la plus grande île du Lac Yellowstone, sert de refuge aux oiseaux aquatiques et aux aigles qui se nourissent de truites.

Frank Island, die größte Insel im Yellowstonesee, bietet ein Zuhause für viele Arten von Wasservögeln und sogar für weißköpfige Seeadler, die einheimische *Cutthroat* - Forellen im See fangen.

イエローストーン湖で最大の島フランクアイランド（フランク島）は湖にいるカットスロート鱒を餌とする多くの水鳥やはげ鷲の生育地となっている。

Frank Island, the largest island in Yellowstone Lake, serves as home to many waterfowl and bald eagles that fish for cutthroat trout in the lake.

La Rivière Yellowstone fait un léger détour lorsqu'elle passe par Gardiner, au Montana, juste en dehors de la porte nord du Parc de Yellowstone. La ville de Gardiner a beaucoup prospéré au cours des dernières années car le nombre de touristes ne fait qu'augmenter.

Der Fluß Yellowstone macht eine leichte Biegung, wenn er durch die Ortschaft Gardiner, Montana, fließt, die unmittelbar vor dem Nordeingang des Parks liegt. Die Wirtschaft Gardiners florierte in den letzten Jahren, da die Gemeinde sich auf die Bedürfnisse der Touristen einstellte.

イエローストーン川はイエローストーン北入口のすぐ外側にあるモンタナ州のガーディナーを少しねじりながら流れている。近年、ガーディナーの経済はイエローストーンへの観光客増加と共に繁栄してきている。

The Yellowstone River slightly kinks as it flows through Gardiner, Montana, just outside Yellowstone's North Entrance. Gardiner's economy has boomed in recent years as it caters more to Yellowstone visitors.

Blottie entre deux hautes chaînes de montagnes, la vieille ville minière de Cooke City prospère grace au tourisme. Des sociétés envisagent la réouverture des mines d'or, ce qui changerait beaucoup l'aspect isolé de cette communauté montagnarde.

Das zwischen zwei hohen Bergketten eingebettete Dorf Cooke City, das früher vom Bergbau lebte, blüht heute vom Fremdenverkehr. Bergbaufirmen sind am Überlegen, ob sie die Goldbergwerke wieder öffnen sollen, was den Charakter dieses einsamen Bergdorfs allerdings wesentlich verändern würde.

二つの高い山脈の尾根間の開墾地にある古い鉱山の町クックシティーは今日観光客がもたらす経済で繁栄している。鉱山会社が金鉱の再開鉱を考慮しているが、そうなると、この孤立した山麓の町の特性が変わりうるかもしれない。

Nestled in the cleft of two high mountain ridges, the old mining town of Cooke City now thrives on a tourist-based economy. Mining companies are considering reopening the gold mines, which could change the character of this isolated mountain community.

Une trait de lumière pénêtre les nuages et illumine le bord du Lac Lewis. Lac Lewis est le troisiéme plus grand lac de Yellowstone. Ce lac en forme de coeur est bien connu des pêcheurs de truites.

Ein Sonnenstrahl stielt sich durch die Wolken und beleuchtet das Ufer des Lewissees. Der herzförmige Lewissee ist der drittgrößte See in Yellowstone und ist bei Forellenanglern sehr beliebt.

雲のあいまから一条の光がルイス湖岸を照らす。イェローストーンで三番目に大きいハート型をしたルイス湖は大きなブラウン鱒やレーク鱒を釣るのに絶好の場所である。

A shaft of light leaks through the clouds to illuminate the shore of Lewis Lake. The third largest lake in Yellowstone, heart-shaped Lewis Lake is popular with anglers seeking large brown and lake trout.

Tout ce qui reste du vieux lit de la petite rivière semble fait écho au lit actuel de *Pelican Creek* (Rivière aux Pélicans), en témoignage des changements de la nature.

Als Zeugen des veränderlichen Charakters der Natur scheinen Restteile des alten Bachbettes das gegenwärtige Bett des *Pelican Creek* (Pelikanbach) widerzuspiegeln.

古い小川河床の跡が現在あるペリカンクリークの水路と似かよって見える。これはいかに自然がその水路を変えるかを証明しているようだ。

Remnants of the old creek bed seem to echo off the existing channel of Pelican Creek, testimony of how nature changes course.

Des nuages se reflètent sur *Riddle Lake* (le Lac des Mystères). Autrefois, les trappeurs pensaient que le lac, qui se trouve à 5 kilomètres de *West Thumb* (Pouce de l'Ouest), se déversait à la fois dans l'Atlantique et dans le Pacifique. Le lac n'est qu'à un kilomètre et demi à l'est de la ligne de partage des eaux et ne se déverse que dans le Lac Yellowstone.

Wolken spiegeln sich im *Riddle Lake* (Rätselsee), fünf Kilometer südlich von *West Thumb*. Früher glaubten Fallensteller, daß Wasser aus diesem See in beide Ozeane fließt. In Wirklichkeit befindet sich dieser See eineinhalb Kilometer östlich der nordamerikanischen Wasserscheide und hat Zulauf nur in den Yellowstonesee.

雲の形がリドル湖の水面に反映する。かって猟師達はウエストサム（西の親指）の南約5キロにある湖の水が大平洋と大西洋に流れていると信じていた。この湖はコンチネンタルディバイド（米大陸分水界）から東1.6キロのところにありイエローストーン川だけに流れている。

Images of clouds mirror off the surface of Riddle Lake. Trappers once thought the lake, three miles south of West Thumb, drained to both the Pacific and Atlantic Oceans. The lake is one mile east of the Continental Divide and drains only into Yellowstone Lake.

Silhouetté par le soleil couchant, un nuage de pluie se déverse le long de la bordure est du Parc de Yellowstone. Les orages de fin d'après-midi sont fréquents en été.

Eine sich gegen die untergehende Sonne abzeichnende Wolke regnet sich an der östlichen Grenze des Yellowstoneparks ab. Solche Gewitter am Spätnachmittag sind für Sommerwetter im Park typisch.

日没に影を映し雲がイエロースト ーン公園の東境界線沿いに雨を落 とす。夕ぐれ時の雷雨は夏特有の 天候である。

Silhouetted against the setting sun, a cloud dumps a rain shower along the eastern boundary of Yellowstone Park. Late afternoon thunderstorms are characteristic of summer weather.

Quand la neige fondra de ce plateau sur la ligne de partage des eaux, l'eau coulera à la fois vers le Pacifique et vers l'Atlantique. *Two Ocean Plateau* (le Plateau des Deux Océans) alimente à la fois la *Snake River* (Rivière Serpent) de même que la Rivière Yellowstone.

Wenn der Schnee auf dieser auf der kontinentalen Wasserscheide liegenden Hochebene wegschmilzt, fließt das Wasser in beide Ozeane, den Atlantik und den Pazifik. Zwei Flüsse, der Snake und der Yellowstone, werden vom *Two Ocean Plateau* (Zwei-Ozeane-Plateau) gespeist.

イエローストーン南東部にあるコンチネンタルディバイドプラトー（米大陸分水界高原）の雪が溶ける時、その雪溶け水は大平洋と大西洋の両方に流れる。ツーオーシャンプラトー（二大洋高原）はスネーク川とイエローストーン川の両方に水を送っている。

When the snow melts off this Continental Divide plateau in southeastern Yellowstone, it will flow to both the Atlantic and Pacific Oceans. Two Ocean Plateau feeds water to both the Snake and Yellowstone Rivers.

Sur le plateau entre Norris et Canyon, des troncs d'arbres ressemblent à des cure-dents éparpillés. Cet endroit a brûlé intensément pendant l'incendie de 1988. Les arbres étaient tombés il y a plusieurs années et n'ont fait qu'alimenter le brasier.

Verkohlte Baumstämme auf der Hochebene zwischen Norris und Canyon sehen wie verschüttete Zahnstocher aus. Diese Gegend wurde während der Waldbrände 1988 besonders stark betroffen. Die Bäume waren einige Jahre zuvor umgekippt und versorgten nun das Feuer mit viel trockenem Brennmaterial.

ノリスとキャニヨンの間にある高原地帯に火災で丸焦げになった樹木がまるでつまようじのように倒れている。この辺は1988年の森林火災の極度の熱でやけてしまった。火災の数年前、風で吹き倒され乾燥した樹木が燃料となり大火となった。

Charred logs resemble spilled toothpicks on the plateau between Norris and Canyon. This area burned with intense heat during the forest fires of 1988. The trees had been blown down several years earlier and provided dry fuel for the raging fires.

Old Faithful, the world's most famous geyser, erupts to an audience of thousands of people every day. For many visitors to Yellowstone, traveling to see Old Faithful is as much a pilgrimage as a trip.

Old Faithful (le Vieux Fidèle), le geyser le plus connu du monde, fait éruption chaque jour devant des milliers de spectateurs. Pour beaucoup de visiteurs qui se rendent à *Old Faithful*, cela représente autant un pélérinage qu'un voyage de plaisir.

Old Faithful, der berühmteste Geiser der Welt, eruptiert jeden Tag vor Tausenden von Zuschauern. Für viele Parkbesucher bedeutet der Ausflug zum *Old Faithful* beinahe eine Pilgerfahrt.

世界で最も有名な間欠泉であるオールドフェイスフルは日ごと訪れる何千人もの観光客を前に噴き上げる。イエローストーンを訪れる観光客にとってオールドフェイスフルを見物することは巡礼の旅のようなものである。

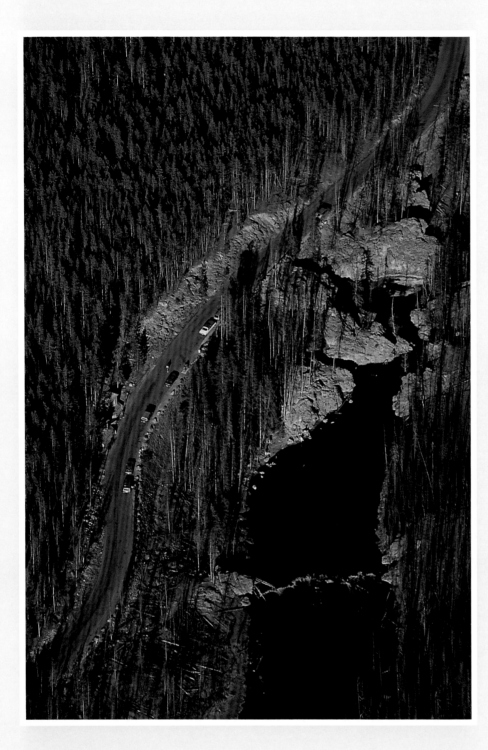

L'eau chaude des formations thermales telles que les sources chaudes et les geysers, réchauffent suffisamment la *Firehole River* (Rivière des Trous de Feu) pour qu'elle soit assez bonne pour y nager. La plupart des rivières de Yellowstone prennent leur source près des neiges et sont beaucoup trop froides pour la natation et aujourd'hui, il est interdit de nager dans les régions thermales.

Wasser aus heißen Quellen und Geisern wärmt den *Firehole River* (Fluß Feuerloch) genug, um Schwimmen zu ermöglichen. Die meisten Flüsse in Yellowstone quellen aus schmelzendem Schnee und sind daher zu kalt zum Schwimmen. Außerdem ist Schwimmen in den Thermalgebieten nicht gestattet.

温泉や間欠泉などの熱水源口から出る熱水がファイヤーホール川を暖め泳ぐのにも快適である。イエローストーンにあるほとんどの川は雪溶けが流れているので泳ぐには冷たすぎるし、熱水地帯での水泳は禁止されている。

Hot water from thermal features such as hot springs and geysers warm the Firehole River enough to make swimming comfortable. Most Yellowstone streams flow from melted snow and are too cold for swimming, and swimming is prohibited in thermal areas.

La Rivière Lewis se déverse d'une des deux cascades d'un canyon à 3 kilomètres au sud du Lac Lewis. Autrefois, les cascades représentaient un obstacle pour les poissons qui remontaient le fleuve jusqu'au Lac Lewis qui restait démuni de poisson. Au début du siècle, la truite y a été introduite.

Der Fluß Lewis stürzt einen der zwei Wasserfälle im Cañon drei Kilometer südlich von Lewis Lake hinab. Die Fälle behinderten früher Fische, die flußaufwärts bis Lewissee zu schwimmen versuchten. Der See blieb unfruchtbar, bis früh in diesem Jahrhundert Fische endlich in den See verpflanzt wurden.

ルイス川がルイス湖南方 3.0 キロにある渓谷の二つある滝の一つに流れている。かってこの滝はルイス湖に向って上流しようとする魚の障害物であり、この湖には1900年代の始めますが移殖されるまで魚がいなかった。

The Lewis River tumbles down one of two waterfalls in a canyon two miles south of Lewis Lake. The falls once served as an obstacle to fish moving upstream into Lewis Lake, which was barren of fish until trout were planted early this century.

Colter Peak (le Sommet Colter) se dresse au dessus de la région la plus fréquentée du parc. Ce sommet de 3.248 mètres a recu son nom de John Colter, un montagnard qui, paraît-il, a été le premier à explorer la région de Yellowstone en 1807.

Colter Peak (Coltergipfel) ragt über die *Thorofare* - Gegend des Yellowstoneparks. Der 3 248 Meter hohe Gipfel wurde nach dem *Mountain Man* John Colter benannt, der 1807 vermutlich der erste Weiße war, der das Yellowstone Gebiet erforschte.

コルター峰がイエローストーンの ソロフェア山脈域にぼんやり浮び 上がって見える。標高3248メート ルの峰は1807年イエローストーン 最初の白人山男ジョン・コルター にちなんで名付けられたものであ る。

Colter Peak looms above the Thorofare region of Yellowstone. The 10,683-foot-high peak is named after mountain man John Colter, believed to be the first white man to explore the Yellowstone area in 1807.

Des ombres s'étirent sur le Lac Yellowstone alors que le soleil se couche derrière une nappe de nuages.

Wenn die Sonne hinter einer Wolkenwand untergeht, verlängern sich die Schatten auf dem Yellowstonesee.

雲にさえぎられた夕日がイエローストーン湖にその影をなげかける。

Shadows begin to stretch across Yellowstone Lake as the sun sets behind a bank of clouds.

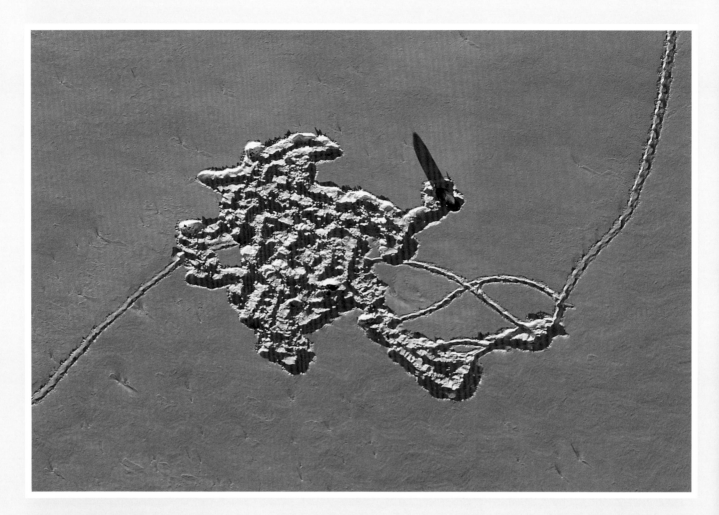

Un bison fait des dessins artistiques dans la neige profonde quand il broute à la Vallée Hayden. Le cou épais de ce bison lui est pratique pour déblayer la neige tout en cherchant sa nourriture.

Ein Büffel prägt ein künstlerisches Muster in den tiefen Schnee ein, während er im Haydental weidet. Der kräftige Nacken der Büffel ist dazu geeignet, bei der Futtersuche den Schnee wegzuräumen.

バイソン（バッファロー）がヘイデンバレー（ヘイデン渓谷）で草を食べる時、深い雪の中に芸術的な模様を描く。このバイソンの太い首が餌をあさる時、雪を押し退けるのに便利なのである。

A bison creates an artistic pattern in the deep snow as it grazes in the Hayden Valley. The thick neck on this bison is handy for pushing away snow while foraging.

Des bisons broutent le long du lit d'une rivière près de *Canyon Village*. Plus de 2.800 bisons se promènent dans le parc en trois troupeaux distincts.

In der Nähe von *Canyon Village* grasen Büffel ein Flussbett entlang. Über 2 800 Büffel ziehen in drei Herden in Yellowstone herum.

バイソン（バッファロー）がキャニオンビレッジ（渓谷村）近くの河畔で草を食べている。2800頭以上ものバイソンは三つの群れに分れて移動して回る。

Bison graze along a streambed near Canyon Village. More than 2,800 bison roam Yellowstone in three separate herds.

Lake Hotel (l'Hôtel du Lac) domine le Lac Yellowstone. Ce lac a une circonférence de 176 kilomètres et est alimenté par 140 affluents. Chaque année 500.000 truites y servent de nourriture aux pélicans, aux grizzlis, aux martres, aux mouettes et aux canards.

Der *Lake Hotel* -Komplex überblickt den Yellowstonesee, der eine 176 Kilometer lange Uferlinie und 140 Nebenflüsse hat. Jedes Jahr werden 500 000 einheimische *Cutthroat* - Forellen aus diesem See von Pelikanen, Grizzlybären, Möwen, Nerzen und Enten aufgefressen.

レイクホテル一帯の宿泊設備がイエローストーン湖を見渡す位置にある。この湖はその湖岸線が176キロもあり、140もの支流が流れている。毎年湖にいる50万匹ものカットスロート鱒がペリカン、グリズリー熊（灰色熊）、ミンク、かもめそして鴨の餌となっている。

The Lake Hotel complex overlooks Yellowstone Lake. The lake has 110 miles of shoreline and has 140 tributaries. Each year, 500,000 cutthroat trout in the lake serve as food for pelicans, grizzly bears, mink, gulls and ducks.

Le majestueux *Lake Hotel* (Hôtel du Lac) est perché sur la rive nord du Lac Yellowstone. Construit en 1891 et rénové dans les années 1980, l'hôtel offre aux touristes les chambres les plus élégantes du Parc de Yellowstone.

Das prächtige *Lake Hotel* steht am Nordufer des Yellowstonesees. Im Jahre 1891 gebaut und in den achtziger Jahren renoviert, bietet das Hotel die eleganteste Unterkunft im ganzen Park.

壮厳なレイクホテルはイエロース トーン湖の北湖畔にある。1891年 に建てられ、1980年代に改造され たこのホテルはイエローストーン では最も優雅な宿泊設備である。

The majestic Lake Hotel is perched along the northern shore of Yellowstone Lake. Built in 1891 and remodeled in the 1980s, the hotel offers the most elegant overnight accommodations in Yellowstone.

Les bâtiments de
l'administration centrale du
Parc National de Yellowstone
se trouvent à la base des
Mammoth Hot Springs (Sources
Chaudes de Mammouth).
Aujourd'hui, la communauté
s'appelle *Mammoth* mais de
1891 à 1918 c'était un poste
avancé de l'armée américaine
connu sous le nom de *Fort
Yellowstone.*

Die Hauptstelle der
Yellowstone
Nationalparkverwaltung ist
unten an den *Mammoth Hot
Springs* (Riesige Heiße
Quellen) gelegen. Die Ortschaft
heißt heute *Mammoth*, aber
von 1891 bis 1918 war sie ein
Vorposten der US Armee
namens *Fort Yellowstone.*

イエローストーン国立公園庁本部
がマンモスホットスプリングの麓
に位置する。この辺は今日では
マンモスと呼ばれているが、1891
年から1918年までは陸軍司令部の
フォートイエローストーンとして
知られていた。

Headquarters for Yellowstone
National Park lies at the base
of Mammoth Hot Springs. The
community is now called
Mammoth but from 1891 to 1918
it was an outpost of the U.S.
Army known as Fort
Yellowstone.

La Rivière Bechler descend un escalier de cascades au sud-ouest de Yellowstone, région connue aussi sous le nom de *Cascade Corner* (Coin des Cascades). On peut trouver jusqu'à 21 cascades importantes dans ce coin perdu de Yellowstone.

Der Fluß Bechler im südwestlichen Yellowstone stürzt eine Treppe von Wasserfällen hinab. Da sich 21 bedeutende Wasserfälle in dieser Ecke des Parks befinden, wird das Gebiet *Cascade Corner* (Kaskadenecke) genannt.

ベチラー川はカスケードコーナーという名でも知られているイエローストーン南西部にある段層のように連なる滝を落下する。21もの滝がこの山深いイエローストーンの場所で見られる。

The Bechler River steps down a staircase of waterfalls in southwestern Yellowstone, also known as "Cascade Corner." Twenty-one major waterfalls can be found in this remote corner of Yellowstone.

Grant Village, une des constructions les plus récentes et plus controversées du parc, se trouve sur la rive ouest du Lac Yellowstone. Là, on peut y trouver un magasin, un musée, une station-service et des chambres d'hôtel.

Das *Grant Village*, die neueste Siedlung im Park, befindet sich am Westufer des Yellowstonesees. Die Ortschaft bietet Einkaufsmöglichkeiten, ein Museum, eine Tankstelle und Unterkunft an.

公園内で最も新しく、時折り問題とされている開発地のグラントビリッジ（グラント村）はイエローストーンの西湖岸沿いにある。売店、博物館、給油所、宿泊施設が備わっている。

Grant Village, the park's newest and sometimes controversial development, is along Yellowstone Lake's western shore. The development includes a store, museum, service station and overnight rooms.

Un arc-en-ciel émerge de nuages orageux et transperse la surface du Lac Yellowstone. Le lac a une superficie de 35.000 hectares et la température moyenne de l'eau est de 5 degrés C. Les tempêtes y sont fréquentes et violentes; il peut être dangereux d'y faire du bateau.

Ein Regenbogen erstreckt sich aus Sturmwolken bis an die Oberfläche des Yellowstonesees. Dieser See breitet sich über 35 000 Hektar aus und hat eine durchschnittliche Wassertemperatur von fünf Grad. Heftige Stürme brechen oft aus, so daß Bootfahren manchmal gefährlich ist.

嵐雲からの虹がイエローストーン湖の水面にさしこむ。この湖の水面積は 348 平方キロメートル、平均水温は 5 度である。しばしば荒々しい嵐がおき舟遊びをするのに危険なこともある。

A rainbow shoots from storm clouds to pierce the surface of Yellowstone Lake. The lake covers 136 square miles and has an average water temperature of 41 degrees. Storms are frequent and fierce, and boating at times can be hazardous.

Des logements pour voyageurs s'étendent à travers la forêt à *Canyon Village*, situé près du Grand Canyon de Yellowstone. Par une nuit d'été typique, des centaines de visiteurs passent la nuit dans des cabanes ou dans des chambres d'hôtel à Canyon.

Unterkünfte für Gäste wuchern durch den Wald bei *Canyon Village* in der Nähe vom Grand Canyon von Yellowstone. In einer typischen Sommernacht schlafen Hunderte von Gästen in Hütten und Zimmern bei Canyon.

イエローストーンのグランドキャニオン近くにあるキャニオンビリッジ（渓谷村）では宿泊設備が森林の中ほうぼうに広がっている。典型的な夏の夜は何百人もの客がキャニオンにあるキャビンやら宿泊室に泊まる。

Guest lodging sprawls through the forest at Canyon Village, located near the Grand Canyon of the Yellowstone. On a typical summer night, hundreds of guests stay in the cabins and rooms at Canyon.

Entourée de terres appartenant au gouvernement, la ville de *West Yellowstone* est le portail du Parc de Yellowstone. Pendant l'hiver, la ville est envahie de motoneiges. Les habitants ont surnommé leur ville "Capitale Mondiale du Motoneige".

Umschlossen von staatlichen Wäldern dient die Kleinstadt *West Yellowstone* als Eingang zum Yellowstone Nationalpark. Im Winter brummen dort Schneefahrzeuge herum, und die Einwohner haben ihr Städtchen zur „Schneefahrzeughauptstadt der Welt" erklärt.

四方を連邦領土に囲まれた町ウエストイエローストーンはイエローストーン公園への通路の町として重要な役割を果している。冬の間はスノーモービルの音で賑わい地元ではこの町のことを「世界のスノーモービル首都」と呼んでいる。

Hemmed in by federal lands on four sides, the town of West Yellowstone serves as a gateway community to Yellowstone Park. During winter, the town buzzes with the sound of snowmobiles, and townspeople have proclaimed it the "Snowmobile Capital of the World."

Ridges rise with redundancy behind Eagle Peak in the Absaroka Range along Yellowstone's eastern boundary. This rugged high country is some of the best habitat for bighorn sheep in the Northern Rockies.

Des crêtes de montagnes se dressent en surnombre derrière *Eagle Peak* (Sommet des Aigles) dans la chaîne de montagnes des Absaroka à la frontière est du parc de Yellowstone. Ce terrain élevé et rugueux procure un habitat excellent pour les moufflons des *Northern Rockies* (des Rocheuses du Nord).

Weitschweifige Bergrücken im Absarokagebirge entlang der östlichen Grenze des Yellowstoneparks ragen in den Himmel hinter *Eagle Peak* (Adlerspitze). Dieses hochgelegene und schroffe Gebiet ist ein vortrefflicher Bereich fur die Großhornschafe der Northern Rockies (Nordfelsen).

イエローストーンの東境界線に沿うアブサロカ山脈の山腹にあるイーグルピークの後方に尾根が限りなく連なる。この辺の高山地帯は北ロッキー山脈でもビッグホーンシープ（大角山羊）の生育地として有名である。

La Rivière Gardner suit un cours sinueux en passant par *Gardner's Hole* (Trou de Gardner), au sud de l'administration centrale du Parc à Mammoth. Les hommes des montagnes appelaient souvent les vallées des "trous".

Der Fluß Gardner windet sich durch *Gardner's Hole* (Gardnerloch), südlich von der Hauptstelle der Parkverwaltung in *Mammoth*. *Mountain Men* (frühe Fallensteller, die häufig unter den Indianern lebten) nannten Bergtäler oft *holes* (Löcher).

ガードナー川がマンモスにある公園庁本部の南方にあるガードナホールをつきぬけ曲がりくねって流れている。山男達はしばしば渓谷のことを「ホール」と名付けた。

The Gardner River travels a serpentine track through Gardner's Hole, south of park headquarters at Mammoth. Mountain men often labeled mountain valleys as "holes."

Des nuages recouvrent la *Firehole River* (Rivière des Trous de Feu) et les sources chaudes. Étant le plus grand bassin géothermal du monde, le Parc de Yellowstone comprend plus de 10.000 formations hydrothermiques y compris les sources chaudes, les geysers et les fumerolles.

Wolken bedecken den *Firehole River* (Fluß Feuerloch) und dampfende heiße Quellen. Als größtes geothermales Gebiet der Welt hat Yellowstone insgesamt über 10 000 hydrothermale Naturerscheinungen, einschließlich heißer Quellen, Geiser und Fumerolen.

ファイヤーホールと蒸気を噴出する温泉地帯一面に雲が覆う。世界最大の地熱活動域のイエローストーン公園には一万以上もの温泉、間欠泉、噴気孔などの熱水地帯がある。

Clouds blanket the Firehole River and steaming hot springs. The largest geothermal basin in the world, Yellowstone Park has more than 10,000 hydrothermal features, including hot springs, geysers and fumaroles.

Des arcs-en-ciel scintillent dans la brûme de *Lower Falls* (Cascades du Bas). *Lower Falls*, avec une élévation de 94 mètres est la cascade la plus haute de Yellowstone. Elle a inspiré beaucoup d'artistes, y compris Thomas Moran.

Regenbogen leuchten aus dem Nebel der *Lower Falls of the Yellowstone* (Untere Wasserfälle des Yellowstone). Mit 94 Metern sind die *Lower Falls* die höchsten Wasserfälle in Yellowstone. Als solche haben sie Künstler wie Thomas Moran inspiriert.

虹がイエローストーン川のローワーフォールズ滝からでる水しぶきの中で輝やく。94メートルの高さから落下するローワーフォールズ滝はイエローストーンで一番高くトーマスモーランをはじめ多くの芸術家たちに感化を与えてきた。

Rainbows shine from the mist of the Lower Falls of the Yellowstone River. At 308 feet, the Lower Falls is the highest waterfall in Yellowstone, lending inspiration to many artists including Thomas Moran.

A *Upper Falls* (Cascades du Haut), l'eau forme une chute de 33 mètres. Durant les grandes eaux en juin le débit est de 1.764 mètres cube par seconde.

Wasser stürzt 33 Meter über die *Upper Falls of the Yellowstone* (Obere Wasserfälle des Yellowstone) hinab. Bei typischer Fluthöhe im Juni strömen mehr als 1 764 Kubikmeter Wasser über die Fälle.

イエローストーン川にあるアッパーフォールズ滝の水が33メーターの高さから落下する。ふだん水量がピークになる六月には1秒間に1764立方センチの水量が流れる。

Water plunges 109 feet over the Upper Falls of the Yellowstone River. During typical peak river flows in June, more than 63,000 cubic feet of water passes over the falls each second.

Au nord-est de Yellowstone, le sommet d'Abiathar, haut de 3.332 mètres, est un des premiers sommets à recevoir les rayons du soleil à Yellowstone.

Der 3 332 Meter hohe *Abiather Peak* (Abiathergipfel) in der nordöstlichen Ecke des Parks empfängt einige der ersten Sonnenstrahlen in Yellowstone.

イエローストーン北東隅にある標高3332メーターのアビアサー峰に朝日が一番に輝やく。

Standing 10,928 feet high in Yellowstone's northeastern corner, Abiathar Peak catches some of the first rays of sunlight to strike Yellowstone Park.

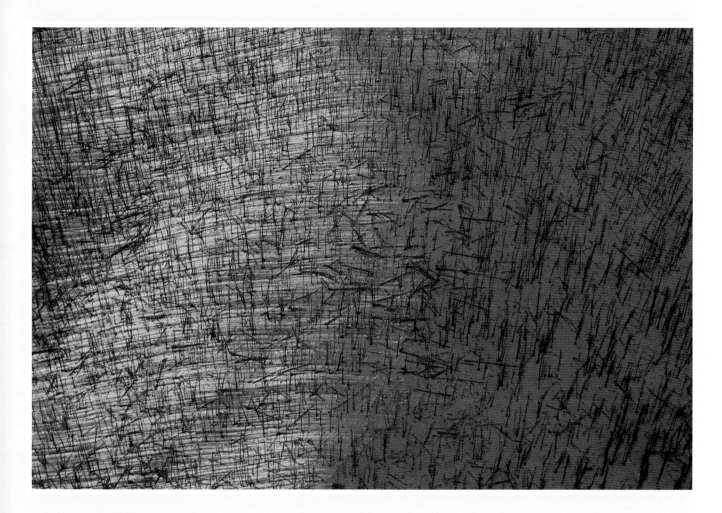

Des arbres carbonisés
ressemblant à des allumettes
brûlées contrastent avec la neige
durant le long hiver de
Yellowstone. Le feu a toujours
fait partie du cycle écologique
de Yellowstone. Cette région
donnera lentement naissance à
une forêt jeune et vibrante.

Während des langen
Yellowstonewinters stehen
verkohlte Baumstämme wie
schwarze Streichhölzer in
starkem Gegensatz zu dem
weißen Schnee. Feuer ist
immer ein Teil des ökologischen
Zyklus in Yellowstone gewesen.
Dieses Gebiet wird allmählich
einen jungen dynamischen Wald
gebären.

長いイエローストーンの冬、焼け
焦げた樹木が雪と対照的に荒涼と
マッチ棒のように立っている。イ
エローストーンでは火災は常に生
態学循環の一環であった。この地
域はゆっくり時間をかけて若く力
強い森林地帯を再生することだろ
う。

Charred trees stand like
matchsticks in stark contrast to
the snow during Yellowstone's
long winter. Fire has always
been part of the ecological cycle
in Yellowstone. This area will
slowly give birth to a young,
vibrant forest.

Nichés sur *Mirror Plateau* (le Plateau Isolé des Miroirs), les bassins de *Rainbow Springs* (Sources aux Arcs-en-ciel) et des *Hot Springs* (Sources Chaudes) miroitent au lever du soleil, avec les Absaroka qui se dressent en arrière plan.

Die im einsamen *Mirror Plateau* (Spiegelplateau) eingebetteten *Rainbow Springs* und *Hot Springs Basin Group* (Regenbogenquelle und Heiße Quellenbecken Gruppe) schimmern bei Sonnenaufgang, während das Absarokagebirge sich im Hintergrund erhebt.

後方にアブサロカ山脈が聳えたち山麓深い処にあるレインボー・スプリング(レインボー温泉)とホットスプリングベイスングループ(温泉盆地群)から出る蒸気が日の出に照らされて揺れ動く。

Nestled on the remote Mirror Plateau, Rainbow Springs and the Hot Springs Basin Group shimmer at sunrise as the Absaroka Mountains rise in the background.

De la vapeur s'échappe et se change en nuages à *Potts Hot Springs Basin* près de *West Thumb* (Pouce de l'Ouest) le long du Lac Yellowstone. Des régions thermales telles que celles-ci sont sans cesse en train de changer du fait de tremblements de terre, du vandalisme et bien sûr à cause de l'évolution géologique naturelle.

Dampf quillt empor und wird zu Wolken im *Potts Hot Springs Basin* (Potts Heiße Quellen Becken) bei *West Thumb* am Yellowstonesee. Heißwassergebiete wie diese werden ständig durch Erdbeben, Vandalismus und geologische Vorgänge verändert.

イエローストーン湖岸沿いウエストサム近くのポッツ温泉域からの蒸気が上昇して雲となる。このような熱水地帯は地震、自然破壊者、そして地質現象により常に変化している。

Steam rises to become clouds at Potts Hot Springs Basin near West Thumb along Yellowstone Lake. Thermal areas such as this are constantly changing because of earthquakes, vandalism and natural geologic processes.

A *Roosevelt Lodge* (Hôtel Roosevelt) à *Tower Junction*, un des concessionaires du parc utilise les chevaux pour les promenades équestres et voyages en charrettes dans les endroits éloignés du parc.

Pferde im Korral bei *Roosevelt Lodge* in *Tower Junction* (Tower-Kreuzung) werden für Reitausflüge ins Hinterland und Wagenfahrten benutzt, die von einem der Parkkonzessionäre angeboten werden.

タワージャンクションにあるルーズベルトロッジで囲いの中にいる馬はイエローストーン公園内で特権を持った民間経営者によるバックカントリー馬乗り（奥地への馬乗り）やワゴン乗り用に使用されている。

Horses corraled at Roosevelt Lodge at Tower Junction are used for backcountry horse and wagon trips provided by one of the park concessionaires.

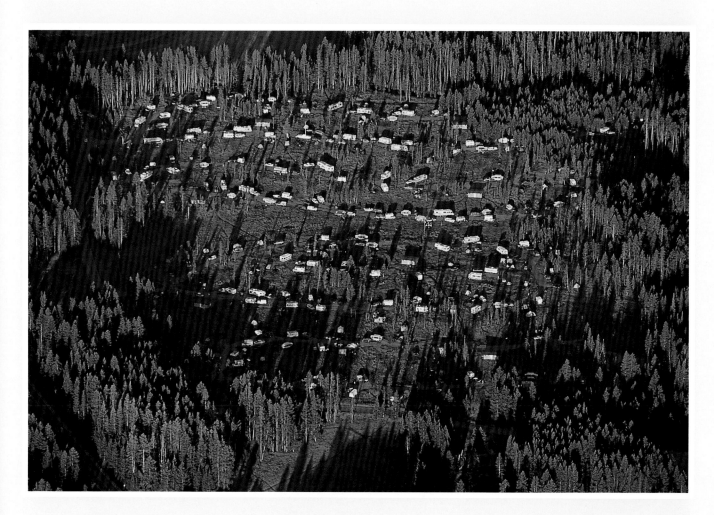

Un village sur roues apparaît la nuit dans une clairière nommée *Bridge Bay Campground* (Camping de la Baie du Pont). Situé près du Lac Yellowstone, le camping est souvent traversé par des bisons et des élans qui broutent entre les camionettes de camping.

Eine Stadt auf Rädern namens *Bridge Bay Campground* bildet sich jeden Abend in einer Lichtung. Dieser Campingplatz in der Nähe des Yellowstonesees wird oft von Büffeln und Elchen besucht, die zwischen den Wohnwagen grasen.

車でくるキャンパー達が夜ごと森林を開拓してつくられたブリッジベイキャンプ場に集まる。イエローストーン湖近くにあるこのキャンプ場にはしばしば車間をぬって草を食べるバイソン（バッファロー）やムース（おお鹿）が訪れる。

A community on wheels forms nightly in a forest clearing called Bridge Bay Campground. Located near Yellowstone Lake, the campground is often visited by the bison and moose that graze between the recreational vehicles.

La teinte bleu foncé de la *Grand Prismatic Spring* (Grande Source en Forme de Prisme) (photo du haut) n'est qu'une parmi plusieurs régions thermales du *Midway Geyser Basin* (Bassin de Geysers du centre) qui s'étend sur plus d'un kilomètre le long de la *Firehole River* (Rivière des Trous de Feu).

Die tiefblaue *Grand Prismatic Spring* (Große Prismatische Quelle), im Bilde oben, ist eine von vielen thermalen Naturerscheinungen im *Midway Geyser Basin* (Mittleres Geiserbecken), die sich eineinhalb Kilometer den *Firehole River* (Fluß Feuerloch) entlang erstrecken.

深紺色のグランドプリスマティック温泉はファイヤーホール川沿い1.6キロに広がるミッドウェイ間欠泉域にある多くの熱水地帯の一つである。

The deep blue hue of Grand Prismatic Spring (top) is one of many thermal areas in the Midway Geyser Basin, which extends for a mile along the Firehole River.

Des voiliers, des yachts et des petits bateaux à moteur sont ancrés à *Bridge Bay Marina* (au Port de la Baie du Pont) le long de la rive nord du Lac Yellowstone. Le port est dans une petite baie protégeant les bateaux en cas d'intempérie.

Segelboote, Kajütboote und kleine Motorboote legen in dem *Bridge Bay Marina* (Yachthafen) am Nordufer des Yellowstonesees an. Dieser Yachthafen ist in einer kleinen Bucht gelegen, die Boote vor dem manchmal rauhen Seewetter schützt.

セールボート、遊航船そして小型モーターボートがイエローストーン湖北岸沿いのブリッジ・ベイマリーナにとめられている。このマリーナは小さな湾の中にあり、時折り来る湖の荒々しい気候からボートを守っている。

Sailboats, cabin cruisers and runabouts park at the Bridge Bay Marina along Yellowstone Lake's northern shore. The marina is in a small bay, protecting boats from the sometimes harsh lake weather.

Près de sa source, la Rivière Madison traverse un canyon à l'ouest du parc. Les incendies de 1988 ont réussi à sauter par dessus ce canyon.

Ganz in der Nähe seiner Quelle, fließt der Fluß Madison im westlichen Teil des Yellowstoneparks durch einen Cañon. 1988 sprangen Flammen der Waldbrände quer über diesen Abgrund.

マディソン川が公園西部にある水源近くのキャニオン（峡谷）をついて流れる。1988年の森林火災はこの峡谷を飛び越えて行った。

The Madison River flows through a canyon near its source in the western portion of the park. Forest fires in 1988 jumped across this canyon.

L'eau jaillissant du sol forme les gigantesques *Mammoth Hot Springs* (Sources Chaudes de Mammouth) près du centre administratif du parc. L'eau venant de quelques centaines de sources coule à raison de 1.890 litres par minute, déposant chaque jour deux tonnes de pierre à chaux donnant aux sources chaudes leur forme de terrace.

Neben der Parkverwaltung in Mammoth hat aus der Erde sickerndes Wasser massive Thermalquellenterrassen aus Travertin geformt. Ungefähr 1 890 Liter Wasser fließen pro Minute aus einhundert Heißquellen. Jeden Tag werden 1 800 Kilogramm terrassenformender Travertin abgelagert.

公園庁本部近くにあるマンモス温泉域から蒸気が上昇する。この辺にある100もの温泉から毎分**1890**リットルもの水が湧き出、温泉段丘を作っている石灰華が毎日２トンも沈殿している。

Water percolating from the ground forms the giant Mammoth Hot Springs near park headquarters. About 500 gallons of water flow per minute from the 100 springs here, each day depositing two tons of travertine limestone that forms the terraced hot springs.

Shoshone Lake glimmers at sunset. Yellowstone's second largest lake, Shoshone covers more than 8,000 acres and is the largest lake in the contiguous 48 states that cannot be reached by road.

Le Lac Shoshone miroite au coucher du soleil. Le Lac Shoshone, le deuxième plus grand lac de Yellowstone a une superficie de plus de 3.200 hectares ce qui le fait le plus grand lac des 48 états contigus d'Amérique du Nord, qui ne puisse être atteint par la route.

Der Shoshonesee schimmert bei Sonnenuntergang. Als Yellowstones zweitgrößter See bedeckt Shoshonesee mehr als 3 200 Hektar. Er ist auch der größte See in den 48 aneinandergrenzenden Staaten zu dem keine Straße führt.

ショション湖が日没時うっすらと照らしだされる。イエローストーンで二番目に大きいショション湖は3200ヘクターにも及び道路の無い湖では隣接した48州の中で一番大きい湖である。

Le sommet d'*Electric Peak* (Sommet Electrique), 3.342 mètres, se dresse au nord de Mammoth. Des explorateurs l'ont nommé ainsi après avoir été forcés d'en descendre par un violent orage en 1872.

Der *Electric Peak* (Elektrischer Gipfel) ragt nördlich von Mammoth 3 342 Meter in die Höhe. Er erhielt im Jahre 1872 seinen Namen, als Yellowstoneforscher durch ein schweres Gewitter zum Abstieg gezwungen wurden.

標高**3342**メートルのエレクトリックピーク（稲妻の峰）がマンモスの北方に聳え立つ。1872年イエローストーン探険者達がその峰から猛裂な稲妻をともなった嵐の為押し戻された時のことにちなんで名付けられた。

The 10,992-foot-high Electric Peak stands north of Mammoth. It earned its name in 1872 when Yellowstone explorers were forced off the peak because of a fierce electrical storm.

La Rivière Yellowstone serpente jusqu'à son delta et se jette dans le Lac Yellowstone. Sur le côté gauche de la photo on peut voir les arbres qui ont brûlé dans l'incendie de 1988.

Der Fluß Yellowstone schlängelt sich durch sein Delta und fließt in den Yellowstonesee. Die braunen Bäume links verkohlten 1988 während der großen Waldbrände.

イエローストーン川がデルタ地帯をぬってイエローストーン湖に流れ込む。写真左手のちゃ色がかった樹木は1988年の森林火災によって焼けたものである。

The Yellowstone River meanders through its delta and flows into Yellowstone Lake. The brown trees on the left side of the photo burned during the forest fires of 1988.

Le *Norris Geyser Basin* (le Bassin de Geysers de Norris) crache de la vapeur de ses douzaines de formations géothermiques. C'est le bassin le plus chaud et le plus actif du parc. A Norris, à 330 mètres de profondeur, la température de l'eau atteint 240 degrés C.

Im *Norris Geyser Basin* (Norris Geiserbecken) speien Dutzende von hydrothermalen Naturerscheinungen Dampf aus. Norris ist das heißeste und aktivste Gebiet im Park. Wassertemperaturen steigen bis 240 Grad 330 Meter unter der Erde.

ノリス間欠泉域にある数多くの熱水源噴口から蒸気が噴き上がる。公園内で最も温度が高く、ノリス間欠泉の地下 330 メートルのところでも 240 度にもたっする。

Norris Geyser Basin belches steam from dozens of geothermal features. The hottest and most dynamic geyser basin in the park, water temperatures only 1,100 feet beneath the surface at Norris reach 465 degrees.

Norris Geyser Basin, (le Bassin de Geysers à Norris) envoie de la vapeur dans l'air. Bien que sa visite soit souvent négligée par les visiteurs, le Bassin de Geysers de Norris offre les exemples les plus divers de geysers, fumerolles et de sources chaudes à Yellowstone.

Dampf wallt aus *Norris Geyser Basin* (Norris Geiserbecken) empor. Besucher übersehen ihn oft, aber Norris Geiserbecken hat einige der verschiedensten Exemplare von Geisern, Fumerolen und heißen Quellen im ganzen Park.

ノリス間欠泉域の噴気孔から空に蒸気が噴射する。観光客がよく見のがすこのノリス間欠泉域はイエローストーンの間欠泉、噴気孔温泉などのさまざまな熱水活動が見られる絶好な場所である。

Norris Geyser Basin pumps steam into the air. Often overlooked by visitors, Norris Geyser Basin offers some of the most diverse examples of geysers, fumaroles and hot springs in Yellowstone.

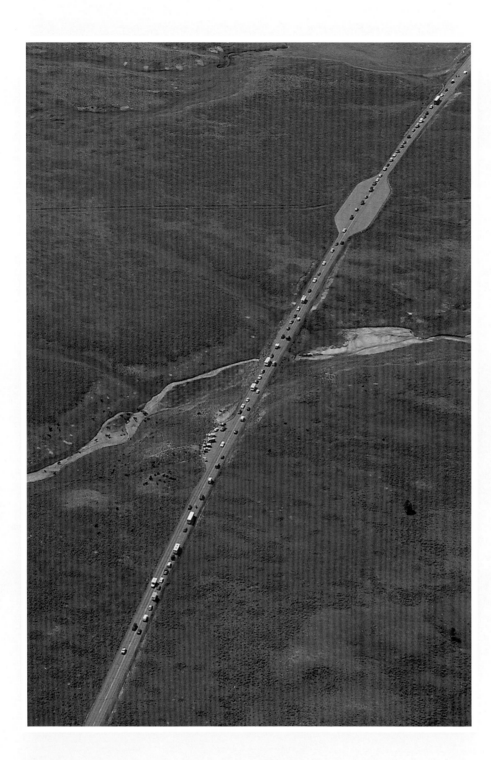

Les bisons broutant à la Vallée Hayden provoquent un embouteillage de proportions gigantesques. Environ 2,5 millions de gens visitent le parc chaque année; beaucoup d'entre eux essaient de capturer la nature sauvage sur film ou vidéo.

Büffel verursachen beim Grasen einen Stau wie im Stoßverkehr. Ungefähr zweieinhalb Millionen Gäste kommen jedes Jahr in den Yellowstonepark. Viele davon versuchen mit Photoapparat oder Videokamera wilde Tiere aufzunehmen.

ヘイデン渓谷で草を食べるバイソン（バッファロー）はラッシュアワー時大きな交通まひの原因となる。年間訪れる 250 万人もの観光客が野生動物の生育をカメラやビデオに収めようとするからである。

Bison grazing in the Hayden Valley cause a traffic jam of rush-hour proportions. About 2.5 million people visit the park each year, many trying to capture wildlife on film or videos.

La Rivière Madison prend sa source à la confluence des Rivières Firehole et Gibbon. Il y a longtemps, des explorateurs ont sans doute discuté de l'avenir de la région à cet endroit même où les campeurs d'aujourd'hui y passent leurs soirées d'été.

Der Fluß Madison entsteht durch den Zusammenfluß des Firehole und des Gibbon. Wo heute Camper ihre Sommerabende verbringen, haben sich frühe Yellowstoneforscher Gedanken über die Zukunft des Gebietes gemacht.

マディソン川はファイヤーホール川とギボン川の合流点から始まる。初期のイエローストーン探険家達は、今日キャンパー達が夏の夜をすごすこの近くの場所で将来のことを語り合ったのかもしれない。

The Madison River begins at the junction of the Firehole and Gibbon Rivers. Early Yellowstone explorers may have discussed the future of the area at this site, near where campers now spend summer evenings.

Les chaînes de montagnes des *Absaroka* (nom indien) et des *Beartooth* (Dent d'Ours) forment une frontière impressionante au coin nord-est du Parc de Yellowstone. Situées juste en dehors de la limite du Parc, elles servent de parcs de loisirs.

Das *Absaroka* - (Indianername) und das *Beartooth*gebirge (Bärenzahngebirge) im nordöstlichen Teil des Nationalparks bilden eine gewaltige natürliche Grenze nach Norden. Diese dicht an der Parkgrenze liegenden Gebirge sind ein beliebtes Erholungsbebiet.

イエローストーン北東部隅にある
アブサロカ山脈とベアトゥス山脈
の巨大な岩塔が群立する。ここは
公園のすぐ外側にありレクリェー
ション場として人気がある。

The Absaroka and Beartooth Mountains stand as a formidable boundary in Yellowstone's northeast corner. Located just outside the park boundary, the mountains serve as a popular recreation area.

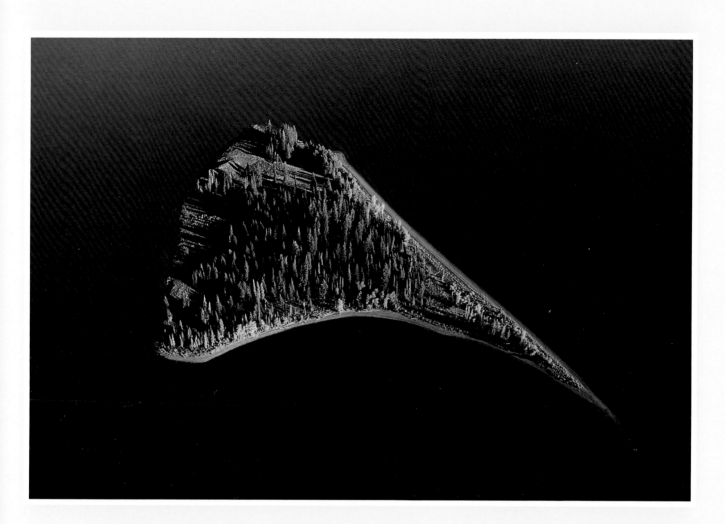

Entourée de gravier, *Dot Island* (l'Ile de la Taille d'un Point), au centre du Lac Yellowstone, pointe vers le sud-est.

Die mit Kies umrandete *Dot Island* (Punkt Insel) zeigt nach Südosten.

砂利に周囲を囲まれたイエロース トーン湖の中央にあるドット島は 南東方向に向いている。

Rimmed with gravel, Dot Island in the middle of Yellowstone Lake points southeastward.

Autrefois, les pêcheurs arrivaient en foule à *Fishing Bridge* (Pont d'où on Pêche), une construction en rondins qui enjambe la Rivière Yellowstone près du Lac Yellowstone. Aujourd'hui, il est interdit de pêcher du pont mais de là, on peut facilement voir les truites.

Früher wimmelte es von Anglern auf der *Fishing Bridge* (Angelbrücke), eine Baumstammkonstruktion, die den Fluß Yellowstone beim Yellowstonesee überquert. Angeln von der Brücke ist nicht mehr gestattet, aber man kann dort immer noch einheimische *Cutthroat* - Forellen beobachten.

かってイエローストーン湖近くのイエローストーン川にかかる丸太作りのフィッシングブリッジは多くの釣師の集まりの場であったが、今では橋からでの釣りは禁じられている。この土地特有のカットスロートますが橋からよく見える。

Anglers once swarmed to Fishing Bridge, a log structure that spans the Yellowstone River near Yellowstone Lake. Fishing off the bridge is now prohibited, but native cutthroat trout are easily seen from the bridge.

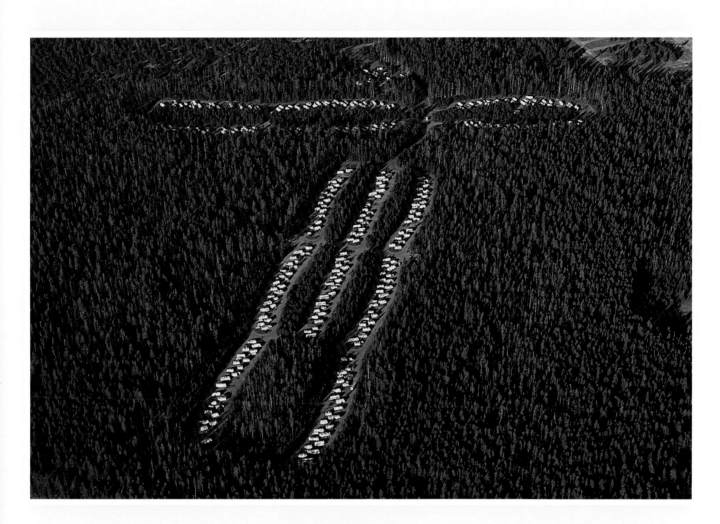

La forêt de pins près du Lac Yellowstone sert de décor au terrain de camping de *Fishing Bridge* (Pont d'où on Pêche). Cet endroit est aussi un chemin souvent traversé par les grizzlis, ainsi qu'un lieu de conflits entre êtres humains et ours.

Der Drehkiefernwald in der Nähe vom Yellowstonesee rahmt den *Fishing Bridge Campground* (Angelbrückecampingplatz) ein. Der Campingplatz befindet sich leider in einem beliebten Bewegungskorridor der Grizzlybären und ist daher Anlaß für einige Konflikte zwischen Menschen und Bären.

イエローストーン湖近くにあるロッジポール松林がフィッシングブリッジ・キャンプ場に相応しい環境を作りだしている。この辺はグリズリー熊（灰色熊）が好んで動き回わる通路でもあり、人間が熊と遭偶する危険な場所でもある。

The lodgepole pine forest near Yellowstone Lake provides the setting for the Fishing Bridge Campground. The area is also a popular travel corridor for grizzly bears and the location of some bear-human conflicts.

Du sommet des montagnes *Table et Turret*, au sud-est du Parc, on a une vue impressionante sur les Tétons dans le Parc National du Grand Téton. De ces sommets, on peut voir les endroits les plus éloignés et isolés du parc.

Die Gipfel von *Table* und *Turret Mountains* (Tischberg und Turmberg) in der südöstlichen Ecke des Yellowstoneparks bieten einen herrlichen Ausblick auf das Tetongebirge im nahegelegenen Grand Teton Nationalpark. Diese zwei Gipfel überblicken einige der abgelegensten Regionen des Parks.

イエローストーン南東隅にあるテーブル山脈とタレット山脈の山頂からはグランドティトン国立公園のティトンが一望に見える。この山頂からは公園内ほとんどの山麓奥地までを見渡すことができる。

The peaks of Table and Turret Mountains in the southeastern corner of Yellowstone provide a commanding view of the Tetons in nearby Grand Teton National Park. These peaks overlook some of the most remote backcountry regions of the park.

Cinq petits lacs, appelés *Cygnet Lakes* (Lacs des Petits Cygnes) sont parsemés sur le *Central Plateau* (Plateau Central) au coeur de Yellowstone. On peut fréquemment voir de petits cygnes en traversant Yellowstone.

Fünf kleine Seen im Herzen des Yellowstoneparks namens *Cygnet Lakes* liegen in einer fruchtbaren Wiese des *Central Plateau* (Zentralplateau) verstreut. *Cygnets* ist der englische Name für Schwanjungen, die oft in Yellowstone zu beobachten sind.

シグニット湖と呼ばれている五つの小さな湖はイエローストーン中心点のセントラルプラトー（中央盆地）の青々とした湿地帯に散点している。シグニットとは白鳥のひなの名前でよくイエローストーンで見かけられる。

Five small lakes called the Cygnet Lakes dot a lush meadow in the Central Plateau in the heart of Yellowstone. Cygnets is the name for young swans, which are often seen in Yellowstone.

Des colonnes de vapeur s'élèvent des *Upper and Midway Geyser Basin* (Bassin de Geysers du Haut et du Centre) à West Yellowstone. A 80 kilomètres, les montagnes Teton émergent en arrière plan.

Dampfwolken türmen sich im westlichen Yellowstone über den *Upper and Midway Geyser Basins* (Oberes und Mittleres Geiserbecken) auf. Im Hintergrund zeichnet sich das 80 Kilometer entfernte Tetongebirge ab.

イエローストーン西部にあるアッパーガイザーベイスン（上部間欠泉域）とミッドウェイガイザーベイスン（中部間欠泉域）から水柱が噴き上がる。後手に80キロ離れたティトン山脈がぼんやり見える。

Columns of steam rise from the Upper and Midway Geyser Basins in western Yellowstone. The Teton Mountains loom in the background, 50 miles away.

Au nord du lac Yellowstone et au sud du *Mirror Plateau* (Plateau des Mirroirs), *White Lake*, (le Lac Blanc) et *Tern Lake* (Lac des Sternes) procurent un excellent habitat pour les oiseaux aquatiques, comme les canards, les oies et les cygnes.

Die nördlich vom Yellowstonesee und südlich vom *Mirror Plateau* (Spiegelplateau) liegenden Seen *White Lake* und *Tern Lake* (Weißsee und Seeschwalbensee) bieten eine hervorragende Heimat für Wasservögel, einschließlich Enten, Gänse und Trompeterschwäne.

イエローストーン湖北方、ミラープラトー（鏡の高原）の南にあるホワイト湖とターン湖は鴨、トランペッター白鳥など水鳥の絶好な生育地である。

North of Yellowstone Lake and south of the Mirror Plateau, White and Tern Lakes provide excellent habitat for waterfowl, including ducks, geese and trumpeter swans.

Des arbres sont alignés sur les sommets de coulée volcanique de *Pitchstone Plateau* (Plateau d'où on Lance des Pierres). Les sommets et ondulations que l'on peut voir aujourd'hui ont été formés par une coulée de lave très lente qui s'est refroidie rapidement, tournant en glace les formes qui sont visibles aujourd'hui.

Reihen von Bäumen stehen oben auf erstarrten Lavarücken des *Pitchstone Plateau* im südwestlichen Teil des Yellowstoneparks. Diese Rücken und Wirbel auf der Hochebene wurden aus zähflüssiger Lava geformt, die schnell abkühlte und die heutigen Formen hinterließ.

イエローストーン南西部にあるピッチストーンプラトー（れきせい岩高原）に溶岩の流れてできた尾根の上に樹木が列をなして立っている。この高原の尾根やうず巻形のものは、ゆっくり流れた溶岩が急に冷却され今日見られるような形に凝固されたものである。

Trees stand in rows atop ridges of lava flows on the Pitchstone Plateau in southwestern Yellowstone. The ridges and swirls on the plateau were formed by slow-flowing lava that quickly cooled, freezing the shapes we see today.

Le brouillard du matin tourbillonne au fond de la Vallée Hayden, un des endroits du parc le plus populaire pour observer les animaux sauvages. La rivière y coule à travers une vallée dénudée qui doit son nom au chef de l'équipe qui fit le premier relevé de plans exploratoires de Yellowstone.

Nebel wirbelt am Frühmorgen auf dem Boden des Haydentals, eines der besten Tierbeobachtungsstellen im Park. Der Fluß Yellowstone strömt durch das baumlose Tal, das nach dem Leiter der ersten offiziellen Forschungsexpedition in Yellowstone genannt wurde.

早朝のもやが公園の壮観な野生動物が見られる場所の一つであるヘイデンバレー（ヘイデン渓谷）をはうようにかかっている。イエローストーン川がイエローストーン最初の公式探険調査隊の隊長の名前にちなんで名付けられた木の無い渓谷をついて流れている。

Early-morning fog swirls along the floor of Hayden Valley, one of the park's most spectacular wildlife viewing areas. The Yellowstone River flows through the treeless valley, named after the leader of the first official exploratory survey of Yellowstone.

Pelican Creek (le Ruisseau des Pélicans) méandre à travers la luxuriance de *Pelican Valley* (la Vallée des Pélicans). Région de terrains accidentés et isolés, la Vallée des Pélicans constitue un habitat idéal pour le grizzli ainsi qu'un refuge pour les autres animaux sauvages y compris les coyotes et les pélicans.

Pelican Creek (Pelikanbach) schlängelt sich durch das fruchtbare Pelikantal. Als abgelegenes Hinterland des Yellowstoneparks ist das Pelikantal eine erstklassige Grizzlybärenheimat und auch ein Zuhause für andere wilde Tiere, einschließlich Kojoten und Pelikane.

ペリカン川が青々と茂ったペリカンバレー（ペリカン盆地）を曲がりくねって流れている。イエローストーン山麓深い所にあるペリカンバレーはグリズリー熊(灰色熊)の主要な生育地であり、又コヨーテやペリカンなど野生動物の生育地でもある。

Pelican Creek meanders through the lush Pelican Valley. A remote backcountry area of Yellowstone, Pelican Valley is prime grizzly bear habitat and home to other wildlife, including coyotes to pelicans.

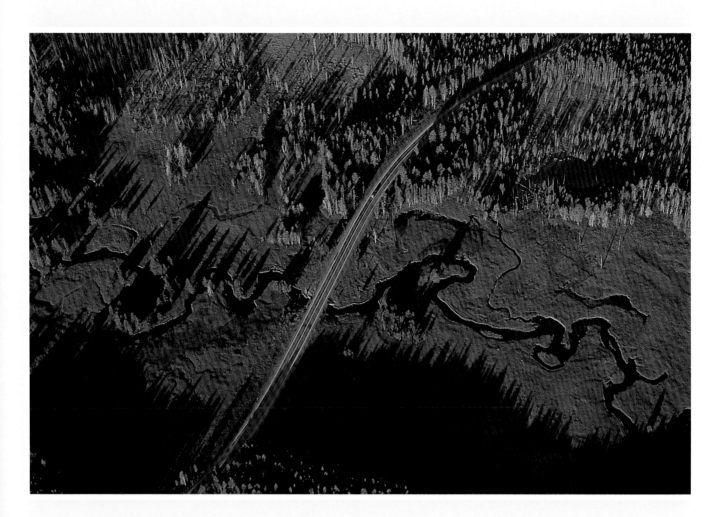

Le trajet serpenté de la Rivière Gibbon contraste vivement avec la route toute droite qui la traverse. Certains des 35.000 wapitis qui passent l'été dans le Parc de Yellowstone fréquentent les prairies le long de la Rivière Gibbon.

Der krumme Lauf des Flusses Gibbon steht in scharfem Gegensatz zu der geraden Landstraße, die ihn überquert.

曲がりくねって流れるギボン川とその上を直線に走る道路とが非常に対照的である。ギボン川沿いの草原には夏の間イエローストーンにいる**35000**頭ものエルク(大鹿)がよく見られる。

The crooked course of the Gibbon River contrasts sharply with the straight line of the road that crosses over it. The meadows along the Gibbon are frequented by some of the 35,000 elk that summer in Yellowstone.

Entouré de neige et recouvert de glace, *Beach Lake* (le Lac bordé de Plages) reflète la solitude de l'hiver à Yellowstone.

Von Schnee umgeben und ganz vereist, spiegelt *Beach Lake* (Strandsee) die Einsamkeit des Winters in Yellowstone wider.

周囲を雪で覆うわれ氷がはりついたビーチ湖はイエローストーンの冬の静寂さを反映する。

Rimmed with snow and plated by ice, Beach Lake reflects winter's solitude in Yellowstone.

Chaque automne, Yellowstone est inondé de couleur, comme celle des peupliers que l'on voit ici, jusqu'aux herbes et roseaux le long des rivières.

Jeden Herbst wird Yellowstone von Herbstfarben überspült, von den hier dargestelten Espen bis zu den Gräsern und Weiden, die entlang der Bäche und Flüße wachsen.

毎年秋になると、イエローストーンはここで見られるように極彩色のアスペン（ポプラ）から川沿りの牧草や柳にいたるまで、秋の色彩色にあふれる。

Every fall, Yellowstone is awash with fall colors, from the brilliant aspens seen here to the grasses and willows along streams.

Roaring Mountain (Montagne mugissante), un flanc de montagne exhalant des fumerolles, réduit la taille des voitures le long de la route entre Mammoth et Norris. Il y a longtemps, des gaz s'échappant de l'eau bouillante sous le sol ont fait mugir la montagne. A cause de changements géologiques, la montagne ne fait plus que siffler.

Roaring Mountain (Heulender Berg), ein Hang voller dampfender Fumerolen, überragt Fahrzeuge auf der Landstraße Mammoth-Norris. Aus kochendem Erdwasser strömende Gase haben früher den Berg heulen lassen. Wegen geologischer Veränderungen zischt er nur noch.

蒸気を吹き出す噴気孔の山腹のローリングマウンティン（ごうごういう山）がマンモスからノリスに続く道を走る車を小さく見せる。かってこの山は煮え立つ地下水からガスが漏れごうごうとうなり声を立てたが、今では地質変化の為シューウという音をたてるだけである。

Roaring Mountain, a mountainside of steaming fumaroles, dwarfs vehicles along the road from Mammoth to Norris. Gases escaping from boiling ground water once caused the mountain to roar. Due to changing geology, Roaring Mountain now only hisses.

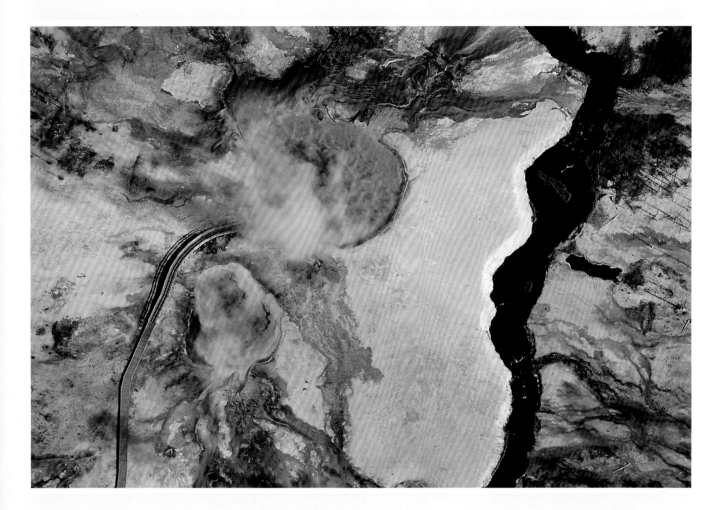

La vapeur s'échappe des sources chaudes au *Black Sand Basin* (bassin de Sable Noir) à côté de *Iron Creek* (Ruisseau ferrugineux). Des fragments d'obsidienne noircissent le sable dans certains coins du bassin et sont plus en évidence à la *Black Sand Pool* (Mare de Sable Noir).

Dampf quillt hoch von heißen Quellen im *Black Sand Basin* (Schwarzes Sandbecken) bei *Iron Creek* (Eiserner Bach). Obsidianbruchteile färben den Sand an vielen Orten des Beckens schwarz und sind im *Black Sand Pool* (Schwarzer Sandteich) am augenfälligsten.

アイロンクリークに隣接するブラックサンドベイスン（黒砂盆地）の温泉から蒸気が噴出する。この辺の盆地では黒曜石の断片が黒い砂に変化する。ブラックサンド池はそれがはっきり出ている。

Steam rises from hot springs at Black Sand Basin, adjacent to Iron Creek. Fragments of obsidian turn the sand black in areas of the basin, and are most evident in Black Sand Pool.